Tasty Food

for

Hasty Folk

LORNA REYNOLDS

Attic Press
Dublin

First Published in 1990 by
Attic Press
44 East Essex Street
Dublin 2

British Library Cataloguing in Publication Data
Reynolds, Lorna
    Tasty food for hasty folk.
    1. Food : Time-saving dishes. Recipes
    I. Title
    641.555.

    ISBN 1-85594-005-1

Cover Design: Luly Mason
Origination: Attic Press
Printing: The Guernsey Press Company Ltd.

In memory of my mother

ABOUT THE AUTHOR

LORNA REYNOLDS, whose life spans the fullness of the 20th century, is one of the most remarkable and distinguished Irish women of her generation. A leading member of the Women's Social and Progressive League in the forties, she was later active in the Anti-Censorship Board - with Maud Gonne presiding at the Inaugural Meeting - and joined the Contemporary Club, where all questions of public and literary interest were hotly debated. It was at a meeting of the Women Writers' Club that she met Kate O'Brien, who became a life-long friend. A brilliant after-dinner speaker, there was hardly a gathering of women in Dublin which she was not invited to address.

Having finished her studies at University College Dublin (where Mary Lavin, Cyril Cusack and Myles na gCopaleen were among her contemporaries) Lorna Reynolds lectured in the English Department there until the mid-sixties when she left Dublin to take up the Chair of Modern English at University College Galway. She has published literally hundreds of critical articles on English and Anglo-Irish literature, co-edited (with Robert O'Driscoll) several volumes in the Yeats Studies Series and recently co-edited the monumental thousand-page *Untold Story - The Irish In Canada*. One of her most recent books is the highly acclaimed *Kate O'Brien: A Literary Portrait*.

Lorna Reynolds's poetry has appeared in many prestigious magazines, including *Botteghe Oscure*, *The Dublin Magazine*, *Poetry Ireland*, *Arena* and others. Representing Ireland at numerous international writers' meetings and conferences, she met many of the most distinguished European writers of the 20th century, such as Simone de Beauvoir, Jean-Paul Sartre, Ignazio Silone, Laxness and Ungaretti.

In 1978, Lorna Reynolds returned to Dublin from Galway, where she continues to write and, of course, to cook. When questioned about the relationship between her personality, her literary work and her cooking, she replies:

> "I am a thorough-going character. Whatever I do, I like to
> do well, and that extends to polishing the silver."

'Duck' said Laurence, sniffing gratefully.

It still surprised her that Laurence, who looked ethereal, should spend so much time when he was not being intellectual in talking and apparently thinking about food ... 'I live' he used to say, 'from meal to meal.'

Elizabeth Bowen *The Last September*

Contents

Weights and Measures

Imperial Weights and Measures
16 ounces (oz) = 1 pound (lb)
20 fluid ounces (fl oz) = 1 pint (pt)
2 pints = 1 quart
8 pints = 1 gallon

Metric Weights and Measures
1,000 grams (gr) = 1 kilogram (kg)
100 millilitres (ml) = 1 decilitre (dl)
1,000 millilitres (ml) = 1 litre (l)
1 centimetre (cm) = 100 millimetres (mm)

Metric Equivalents
1 oz = 28.35 gr
1 lb = 453.6 gr
1 pt = 568.2 ml
1 inch = 2.54 cm
1 fl oz = 28.4 ml

Convenient Conversion to nearest unit of 25
1 oz = 25 gr
4 oz = 100 gr
16 oz (1 lb) = 450 gr
$1/_4$ pt = 150 ml
1 pt = 600 ml

American Equivalents
1 American cup = 8 fl oz or 230 ml
1 American tablespoon = $1/_2$ fl oz or 14 ml
1 American teaspoon = $1/_6$ fl oz or 5 ml
1 American pint = 16 fl oz or 454 ml

Abbreviations

F = degrees Fahrenheit
C = degrees Celsius
g = gas
Tbsp = level tablespoon(s)
Tsp = level teaspoon(s)
oz = ounce
pt = pint
lb = pound
" = inche(s)

Guide to Cooking Terms

Al dente: Slightly firm to the taste.

Amalgamate: To combine (eg: egg yolks and oil)

Aspic: A jelly made with bones of meat, fish or poultry or calf's foot; may be easily bought now in packet form.

Baste: To spoon liquid over food as it cooks.

Béchamel: Basic white sauce.

Court Bouillon: A quickly made vegetable stock: add 1 bay leaf, 2 stalks of celery, an onion, 2 carrots, salt and pepper to water; bring to the boil and simmer for about 20 minutes. A vegetable stock cube may be substituted.

Disjoint: To cut poultry or game into small pieces by dividing at the joint.

Feta Cheese: A Greek cheese. Cheshire may be used as a substitute.

Gratin: To cook 'au gratin' is to brown food in the oven. A gratin dish is an oven-proof dish.

Isinglass: A jelling agent; like gelatine, only powdered.

Lardons: Strips of bacon or diced bacon or pork fat.

Marinade: A highly flavoured liquid in which food is soaked before cooking.

Marinate: To soak food (eg: meat or poultry) before cooking to moisten, tenderise and flavour it.

Poach: To cook gently in simmering (never boiling) water.

Purée: To press food through a fine sieve or food mill. A blender may be used although the effect is not quite the same.

Quenelles: Finely minced or pounded flesh of poultry, game, fish etc; usually mixed with egg white or cream and poached in stock.

Ramekin: Small oven-proof dish, usually earthenware, suitable for individual soufflés, baked eggs etc.

Roux: Amalgamation of butter and flour over gentle heat. Forms the base of many sauces.

Sauté: To fry lightly and quickly in a small quantity of butter or oil.

Steam: To cook food suspended over boiling water or stock. A special steamer may be used or a colander over a saucepan.

Tabasco: Very hot and spicy bottled sauce made from capsicums.

Zest: Very finely-grated rind of orange or lemon.

Foreword

My friendship with Lorna Reynolds goes back to the time of my arrival in University College, Dublin (UCD), from Spain in 1956, as a young assistant in the Department of Spanish.

My first impression on entering Earlsfort Terrace was how totally different it was from my own university in Madrid. It was small, traditional, seemingly unchanging, everybody knew one another, and particularly, everybody knew each other's political affiliations. The College was part of a university which was technically secular but the atmosphere of the place at the time, enhanced by the conspicuous presence of clerical garb both among staff and students, was staunchly Catholic, perhaps in acknowledgement of its connection with Newman's Catholic University. This was not totally unfamiliar, since in 1956 some Spanish institutions shared a similar ambience. In any case, it had nothing to do with the cordiality of my colleagues. There was, however, one curious feature of the Earlsfort Terrace days which astonished me - the ritual segregation of sexes amongst the academic staff.

This segregation was represented by the Lady Professor's Room, a sort of *sancta sanctorum* for the women academics or at least those of them who liked to be secluded and 'protected' from men. It was a spacious room with several comfortable armchairs, an impressive fireplace and a big round table. All occupants wore academic gowns, venerable women Professors were constantly on the telephone, either reading out grocery lists for delivery by Findlaters or chatting to their friends. Observation of the conventions was important and the whole scene was presided over by a large portrait of Professor Mary Hayden above the mantelpiece. Men were not allowed to enter the Lady Professor's Room. Occasional transgressors would come to its threshold but very rarely crossed it.

The Room had certain advantages. One could fix one's garters and discuss such womanly subjects, not many, as were considered to be seemly enough for the delicate ears of the Irish professional middle classes in the 1950s. One could also correct students' papers on one's lap or, with luck, on the round table but, because of the hierarchical nature of the Lady Professors' group, one felt somewhat selfconscious if one succeeded in finding some inches of the table to occupy. Irish women academics had a mild interest in the few foreign members of the group but they were always deliberately nice and tried hard to accustom us to Irish courtesy.

I shall never forget the first time Lorna Reynolds entered this room. To put it mildly, she was different. She breezed in, singularly elegant with a unique and personal style of dress - which she maintains to this day. It was somehow flamboyant and always seemed to include a piece of antique jewellery to complement it. My memory of Lorna in those days is a combination of hats and brooches, browny beige-toned suits and shirt-type blouses, often in pure silk, loose swinging coats and elegant shoes. Unlike the rest of her colleagues, who tended to whisper their views, she spoke in a loud, clear and melodious voice. She was never afraid, as others seemed to be, of being indiscreet. What a blessing this was! There was none of the "mind you I've said nothing" about her. She was always on the record. Her assured manner was always courteous and direct - sometimes it came across as being too direct. She had no fear of committing herself, intellectually or emotionally, to whatever issue was in question. These last two features were most endearing for us foreigners. We were used to them at home and Irish circumlocution could sometimes prove wearisome.

Lorna has always had a great deal of warmth and humanity and she treated even a newly arrived assistant as an equal. A person of open mind, she had a curiosity about new colleagues that was very flattering and she made one feel very much part of the College. Her welcoming manner was sincere because it did not arise out of social compassion for us poor aliens, but from a genuine interest in other nationalities, other points of view and other philosophies of life. Her own originality and, above all, her *joie de vivre* were always intellectually stimulating and appealing.

Lorna's ability to communicate, coupled with her readiness to listen, was a valuable characteristic for her students and friends who remember her enthusiasm and the histrionic ability she brought to her lectures and ordinary conversations alike. Nobody fell asleep when Lorna was speaking! She had, and has, an abiding love of English Literature which she communicated most effectively to generations of students in UCD, and in University College Galway (UCG). All of her students recall her lectures as being exceptionally thought-provoking. In her tutorials she never allowed students to remain impassive or non-committal. There was a story circulating in Earlsfort Terrace about the time she asked a tutorial group, a good few clerics among them, to prepare a sermon on Vanity. One of the young men referred in his particularly well-written essay, prior to the tutorial, to "ladies' powdered faces listening to the words of God and daring to criticise them". He seemingly was afraid to come to the tutorial after that but Lorna sent a message warning him of the dangers of some "powdered faced lady" complaining about him to the bishop!

Lorna proved to be, as well, by her involvement in the Women's Social and Progressive League and in the Women Graduates Association a living assertion of women's rights and independence, a proof of women's contribution to society and an advocate of women's role in the University, a person whose views, openly and forcibly expressed, were distressing and uncomfortable to some of the College authorities. The variety of her commitments and her quixotic unwillingness to leave any injustice unsolved remind me of her mother's words that Lorna recently quoted to me: "Lorna, is it not possible for you, occasionally, to turn the blind eye?" It was a major loss to UCD when the College was unable to retain Lorna's great gifts and originality of thought and the College was the poorer for her departure to University College Galway to take up the Chair of Modern English there.

In addition to her stimulating presence in the Lady Professors' Room, which despite my earlier remarks remains a fond memory, there are some recollections of Lorna that occur to me. They are random, selected in no particular sequence and for no particular reason other than the vividness of her presence in my mind. One of them was a visit my friend and colleague Betty Crowe and myself made to Lorna in the now 'infamous' Torremolinos. Torremolinos was then a pretty village, eight miles on the western side of Malaga and its beach was full of fishing boats. The hotel where Lorna was staying was the *Santa Clara*, built on a cliff that descended to the beach. I remember we passed through olive groves and white arches until we arrived at Lorna's room in one of the several bungalow-type apartments which comprised the annexe to the hotel and dropped by stages to the sea. It was a glorious afternoon, and hot and tired as we were after our ramblings searching for her, we couldn't but laugh when we found Lorna having her siesta covered with a couple of blankets! She often says that the fact that she was born in Jamaica makes her particularly susceptible to the cold but we both thought this was a little excessive ...

I also remember the time she introduced my husband and myself to Kate O'Brien and brought her to our house to dinner. Kate was going to Avila to research the book she published shortly afterwards on Teresa of Avila and I gave her an introduction to an old school friend of mine there. The detailed information I got, after she came back, about my friend's marriage and her impressions of Spain in those days were well worth the introduction! In relation also to Kate O'Brien, I recall vividly the time somebody, with marked lack of success, tried to stop Lorna attending a lecture by Kate O'Brien herself which Lorna had kindly organised. The lecture was in the Shelbourne Hotel and the person at the door objected to Lorna's late arrival on the grounds that the 'house' was full. This was ignored with the words: "I am going in," accompanied by an imperious gesture of Lorna's elegant hand.

And there is still in my memory a garden party with strawberries and cream, many years ago, in her Dublin house when the June weather was less than kind and Lorna, determined that not even the weather was going to defeat her, provided an ample supply of rugs and blankets to keep us warm. Most recently, I remember vividly a trip together, driving down to Limerick with Margaret MacCurtain to the annual Kate O'Brien Weekend where we met some other good friends and when Lorna introduced us to the delights of Verdicchio, one of her favourite wines.

Wine brings me to the end of these few words with a very warm toast of good wishes to Lorna. I have known her for more than thirty years although, since we lived in different parts of Ireland, I was not privileged to share all the secrets of her cooking ability. But reading her book has made my mouth water and brought back more memories of some of Lorna's friends who were in UCD in the 1950s and 1960s and whom I also knew. Because her recipes - more often than not - are tied to loving memories and occasions, and very often to funny anecdotes. I now know well that when a turkey has hung too long, whiskey and more whiskey, in all parts of its anatomy, is the only answer; that you can steam a chicken in a colander if you are on a remote island and if you have a deprived kitchen; that not "everything that comes free is dangerous" as proved by the dead salmon trout that offered itself by the score, after a wild storm off the Arklow coast, to Lorna and her Swedish friend; that what we called Hungarian Goulash is merely a soup in Hungary and finally, that "if the leg of the bird, when wriggled around, does not move easily, the chicken is not ready", to use Lorna's rather graphic description!

Lorna's kind, human nature is also reflected in the wording of her recipes. For example, when she tenderly worries that "a bubble too much of the water might diminish the trout's flavours" and wraps it lovingly in tinfoil and the aromas of herbs and lemon. Or when she transfers her love and affection for everything Mediterranean to every type of meat - beef, lamb, pork - inserting delicate slices of garlic into their most intimate parts. Her concern for the busy cook - the hasty folk of the title - makes her include recipes as easily put together as *Tuna with Leeks and Potatoes* - oh, so quick to prepare in advance and so delicious afterwards, and a beautiful smoked trout mousse I tasted in her own house and will very soon try my hand at. The section on vegetables will teach many of us how to improve this rather neglected lot and there are in the book terrific tips on how to cook them Lorna's way in an aromatic orgy of nutmeg, coriander, caraway seeds, thin strips of green peppers, lemon juice and... very little water. She has brought her own original slant and flair to some traditional recipes, which include the addition of unexpected ingredients to the great benefit of some well known dishes. I have never tasted a more delicious roast lamb than one we shared recently, preceded by the delicious smoked trout mousse I referred to above. I simply cannot wait to use this book and further educate my friends' palates. I intend to try out all the recipes and I shall endeavour to tell Lorna of the results with the same courteous directness that is so characteristic of Lorna Reynolds herself.

Maribel Foley
Dublin
July 1990

Introduction

I have been interested in cooking for as long as I can remember, starting as a small child, when I wedged myself in between the kitchen table and the pots and pans cupboard in my grandmother's house, my chin just reaching the level of the table. I think what fascinated me, to begin with, was the movement of hands to and fro over the table. Hands, that had been given a ritual washing and a thorough drying, moved precisely and decisively among whisks and graters, flour and eggs, lemons and sultanas. Shining bowls and kneading knuckles turned mounds of material out on the wooden boards, put them back and covered them with spotless tea-towels. Whites of eggs were whisked into peaks, butter and sugar beaten to a 'creamy consistency' (I listened as well as watched), lemons and oranges cut in half and squeezed into loosening their juices, spices and herbs measured and chopped. There was a scales but it was seldom used, cups and tablespoons serving as ready reckoners.

The cooker was a big, old, coal range which seemed to me to be rather like the grown ups. It had moods. It grew too hot or too cold very easily. It then had to be cooled off or heated up. Things called dampers had to be opened or shut or adjusted. It hated sudden noises or banging of doors, and if disturbed by any of this, would refuse to do what was required of it. It would fail, for instance, to keep the fruit nicely dispersed through the Christmas cake but would let it all fall to the bottom. This was a trial for the grownups but a wonderful bonus for us children. The collapsed cake would be eaten at once and a new one started. We were not, I am sorry to say, proof against the temptation to 'forget' and accidentally bang a door.

But cooking is associated in my memory not only with such selfish pleasures but also with the traditional Irish pleasure of exercising hospitality. We loved to hear that visitors were invited to lunch or tea. Such ceremonial occasions involved extra care: for lunch, napkins were folded in the shape of a bishop's mitre - a custom going back to Norman times, I learnt many years afterwards - and for tea, the special china and thread-work linen cloths were taken out. Drama and excitement attended on the moment.

The ritual of such meals was an indication that through the appetite has to be gratified, this was not enough. The palate must be pleased, the spirits lifted and the mind stimulated by the food we eat. Fast food may meet the first requirement, but it is far from meeting the others. It hardly takes more time to cook a good simple meal than to open tins and undo plastic wrappings while the taste of the former is infinitely preferable. The sensuous part of our nature is involved in the appreciation of cooking. I have never forgotten the colour of the beetroot - baked, not boiled - by my mother to make a salad. Our earliest memories of colour, taste and smell are bound up with our interest in food - not to mention our emotions - as the famous proustian *madeleine* will serve to remind us.

In due course, I became an academic, not a cook, although my interest in cooking remained intense and over the busy years I put many an inherited, modified or invented recipe to the test. For the most part I had to be quick about what I was doing. I took to the pressure cooker with enthusiasm and I tend to use a covered enamel dish for baking fowl or meat. The dish is easier to clean than the oven.

This cookery book is meant for people in a hurry, most of the time, who enjoy eating good food and who like to, or are driven to, doing the cooking themselves. They might wish to have downstairs that good cook who, in Mrs Beeton's words, 'ought, with the help of the kitchen-maid and the scullery maid, to be able to send up whatever is required', but since 'downstairs' has largely disappeared, they must roll up their sleeves and themselves produce whatever is required.

Time is saved in the kitchen *either* by spending a short concentrated period of preparing and cooking by the quick methods of frying or grilling; the same techniques apply to both - high heat to begin with to sear the meat and a lower heat to cook gently through; *or* by a longer time in the preparation and slow cooking that requires little attention. Pressure-cooking falls in-between, attention being necessary until pressure is reached and the heat lowered. Proper flavouring is essential for all dishes.

Time is also saved by remembering Mrs Beeton's advice: 'a place for everything and everything in its place' and by assembling everything necessary - utensils, instruments, raw materials - before preparation. It also helps to do the cleaner jobs first, so that one does not need constantly to wash one's hands. If I was reduced to only one instrument I think I should settle for a fiercely sharp knife.

I should, perhaps, point out to those who may be worried about their weight that, in spire of what may seem the occasional richness of my recipes, experience would seem to prove that there is no danger of putting on unwanted pounds: my weight has remained constant throughout my adult life - 8st 2lbs to 8st 4lbs.

The recipes offered here are not all-inclusive: they are first and foremost the result of memorable travels and friends and flavoured with personal choice. I often thought I had invented some way of cooking, some combination of ingredients, only to discover later that the French or the Japanese had been doing it for centuries. I can only hope that my prospective readers will enjoy the results of my experiments as much as I myself and my guests do.

Bon appétit!

First Courses

I hate the silly word 'starters' for first courses. It seems completely out of place, as if a meal were a race and one had to be in at the beginning: a meal is a sequence of merging pleasures, leaving one, not jumping up and down with excitement, but nicely tranquillised. When I was a child, the first course always consisted of soup - chicken broth, mutton broth, scotch broth, vegetable soup, or, if you had a bad cold or were recovering from an illness, beef tea. I did not much like any of these except the beef tea, when I was feeling frail. Though I loved the taste of many things, my appetite was capricious. My mother then would ask me what I would like for lunch and I would say, 'Beef tea and toast'.

First courses are meant to whet the appetite not blunt it and soup blunts mine. I make an exception, however, for **Jellied Consommé** served with wedges of lemon. Otherwise, I like sharp, tasty morsels - a mousse of smoked trout, a garlicky pâté, smoked salmon, asparagus with lemon as well as the classic melted butter, a fragment of smoked eel. Soups in tins can be so good and varied that people who hanker after them can easily satisfy themselves by wielding a tin-opener.

If one's main course is of necessity exiguous, then a more substantial first course is in order. I offer the following suggestions:

* A large platter containing several different kinds of tempting morsels, such as black and green olives, the inner stalks of celery or chicory, carrots cut along their length, dolmades (page 26), boiled shrimps, a blue cheese (Cashel for choice), a dip (page 97). Serve with these one or more kinds of crisp bread.
* Danish eggs (page 34)
* Egg Mousse (page 37)
* Small omelette aux fines herbes
* Pasta, of various kinds
* Risotto (page 51)
* Kedgeree
* Various fish mousses (page 27)
* Smoked ham with melon or Salami with figs
* Soused herrings with chives and sour cream

For more evanescent satisfaction I suggest:

* *Melon with port.* Half a melon to each person, the seeds scooped out and the hollow filled with port. This is very popular in Italy.
* *Half an avocado* with some of the flesh scooped out and filled with chopped celery, or chicory, and apple mixed with it and coated with an oil and vinegar dressing.
* *Asparagus* served hot with melted butter or cold with olive oil and lemon juice.
* A *French bean salad* as above, or sprinkled with grated cheese.
* *Angels on Horseback*: prunes, big and juicy, each wrapped around by a rasher of bacon, secured with a cocktail stick and grilled.
* *A tomato and Spanish onion salad.* Tomatoes, skinned and sliced, with the onions sliced very finely and bathed in an oil and vinegar dressing to which a little mustard has been added
* *Half a grapefruit*, either left in its natural condition, or sprinkled with a suspicion of brown sugar and browned under the grill. This is, perhaps, a banal offering but for those who like the sharp taste of grapefruit quite satisfactory.
* Had one 'but world enough and time', *quenelles*, either of fish or vegetable substance, are most delicious, but they do take time.
* *Tomato Jelly*: Tomatoes cut in quarters, skins left on, a little chopped onion, a clove, and a few tarragon leaves if possible; if not, half a teaspoon of dried tarragon; if neither is at hand, substitute marjoram. A dash of salt and black pepper. Cover and simmer gently until the tomatoes are tender; press them through muslin or a nylon sieve to extract the juice, and to every pint add half an ounce of dissolved gelatine. Keep stirring until the mixture begins to cool and then pour it into a jelly mould. Turn out carefully and serve with sliced cucumbers around the base.

Dolmades _____

These are vine leaves stuffed with rice and onions. The vine leaves can be bought in cans but if you wish, you can substitute cabbage leaves for them. Choose York cabbage, firm middle-sized leaves, and drop them into boiling water for 3 minutes or steam for a little longer.

Ingredients

$1/2$ lb chopped onions
$1/2$ cup uncooked rice,
  brown if liked
1 tbsp fine nuts
20 cabbage leaves

$1/8$ pint olive oil
1 tbsp dill or mint
1 cup hot water
1 lemon
Salt and pepper

Method

Heat half the olive oil in a frying pan and sauté the onions until transparent. Add the rice and cook for 5 minutes with a lid on the pan. Add the remaining ingredients except the olive oil, the lemon and the cabbage leaves. Simmer for 5 minutes. Cool. Dry the cabbage leaves and flatten them out. Place a heaped dessertspoon of the filling in centre of each leaf. Make a parcel of each cabbage leaf around the filling. Place them opening-side down in a shallow oven-proof dish. Sprinkle with lemon juice. Add the remaining olive oil and cup of hot water. Do not put too much filling in any one leaf but pack them in tightly together. Cover or place sheet of foil over and cook at 350F, 180C, gas 4 oven for almost 1 hour. Allow to cool in the cooking dish.

Beef Tea

Ingredients

1 lb of round beef
1 pint of cold water

$1/2$ tsp of salt

Method

Discard any fat. Cut up the meat fairly finely. Put into an earthenware jar, add the water and salt, cover lightly and cook in a slow oven, 325F, 170C, gas 3 for three hours. Strain, remove any trace of grease that may float to the surface and serve.

This used to be made in my grandmother's house in the earthenware jar that large quantities of jam or marmalade came in.

Smoked Fish Mousse

Ingredients

4 to 6 oz smoked fish: trout,
   haddock or mackerel
4 tblsps mayonnaise
2 to 3 tblsps cream

1 sorrel leaf finely chopped
Dash of black pepper
Lemon juice to taste.

Method

If haddock is being used it must be first covered with cold water and brought to the boil, taken out and allowed to cool.

Take up your fish, add the mayonnaise and beat well. Next add the cream and continue beating. Season with pepper and add lemon juice carefully to taste. Next chop or cut up the sorrel leaf very finely and incorporate. If you have a blender, all can be done to an ethereal smoothness in a few minutes. Remember the sorrel has a very sharp taste, so be careful. Mix in the lemon juice. Serve in ramekin moulds.

Pâtés

Pâtés of various kinds are to be bought readily nowadays but still a home-made one will have a flavour different from anything you can buy, and by keeping it in the refrigerator for a while the flavour improves. If you want it for a dinner party, you can make it a couple of days in advance. The method is the same whether your pâté is of liver, chicken or fish.

Method

Mince the meat or liver or flake the fish finely. Chop or grind all flavourings finely. Add the seasoning. Put into a bowl and mix all well together. Add the sherry, etc and leave to soak for at least half an hour. Put into a greased oven-proof dish; cover with greased paper; place in a tin of boiling water and bake in a 375F, 190C, gas 5 oven, for 45 minutes.

Liver Pâté

Ingredients

1 lb pork liver, a little lamb, chicken or rabbit liver, as available
$1/_2$ lb fatty bacon
2 medium-sized onions
1 clove of garlic

Lemon juice, ground bay leaves
Thyme, fresh if possible, to taste
A dash of pepper, a soupçon of salt
4 tablespoons medium dry sherry

Chicken, Pigeon or Rabbit Pâté _____

Ingredients

1 lb cooked meat
$1/2$ lb fatty bacon
$1/2$ lb mushroom stalks
1 tsp grated lemon rind
Dash of salt, black pepper and
   nutmeg, a clove of garlic

Lemon, thyme and ground bay
   leaves to taste
2 tbsp of medium dry sherry
2 tbsp of stock in which meat
   was cooked

Fish Pâté _____

Ingredients

1 lb cooked fish, or, at a pinch,
   tinned fish
$1/4$ lb cod's roe, when available
$1/4$ lb bread crumbs
1 tbsp each of lemon juice,
   olive oil, mayonnaise and
   lemon rind

2 tbsp of medium dry sherry
2 tbsp of dry cider
Dash of salt and black pepper

Egg Dishes

I only like eggs as little like eggs as possible, in other words, as omelettes. I can, of course, boil an egg, putting into boiling water from $4^1/_2$ minutes for a soft egg to 10 minutes for a hard one, and I can fry an egg properly, keeping the yolk intact and as soft, or as hard, as you please, and turned or not, as you equally please. But I never do either spontaneously, only when I am asked. I can also poach an egg, which is a more difficult operation, but again only on request.

What I do make without being asked are omelettes. One needs to keep a special pan for them. I have found that an enamel pan is better than a stainless steel one and 7" - 8" diameter the best size. Never try to make a huge omelette. Make two smaller ones instead. One can use almost anything as a filling for an omelette, or one can be purist and keep to an omelette plain, except for some finely chopped herbs. It is difficult, however, to better a cheese omelette.

Cheese Omelette _____

Ingredients

4 medium-sized or 3 large eggs
2 oz cheshire cheese
Walnut-sized knob of butter

2 tbsp water
Salt and pepper to taste
Pinch, liberal, of ground nutmeg

Method

Grate cheese very finely. Cheshire I think best, but failing it, cheddar will do. Break eggs separately into bowl, beat lightly with a fork. Have your pan already on heat, giving it a rub with the merest suspicion of grape-seed oil. Use kitchen paper with a drop of oil on it for this. Add the cold water to the eggs and mix through. Sprinkle in the nutmeg, the pepper and at the last moment, salt. Remember there will be salt in the cheese. Put the small knob of butter on the pan and when it begins to turn brown, pour the eggs in. Take off heat, run a palette knife round the edges and tilt in the liquid egg. When it begins to set, scatter the cheese over the top, put back on heat for a minute. Continue to loosen edges and to fold in the liquidy part. When the top has just set, loosen edges once more and fold omelette over. Serve with a green salad and a dry white wine - a Verdicchio for instance.

Omelette Fillings _____

Instead of cheese, one can use tomatoes, skinned and cooked in butter with a finely chopped garlic clove, or minced chicken with parsley gently heated, or left-over risotto, or a good pâté, or even sausage meat, again gently cooked. Re-heated mushrooms in a cream sauce with garlic make a delicious filling. I once used Cashel blue cheese - it was delectable but something of a strain on the digestion. Asparagus spears make another palatable variation. In fact the possibilities are endless, once you know the basic recipe.

I still pride myself on the fact that Ignazio Silone when he stayed briefly in the West of Ireland with Darina, his wife, and tasted my omelette, told me that I could earn my living as a chef in Paris!

Scrambled Eggs

I discovered, when friends stayed the night after a party, that scrambled eggs go far towards curing a hangover. With the addition of ham or tongue or chicken, all chopped and heated first in the butter, scrambled eggs make quite a substantial dish. You may need more butter, if you attempt this.

Ingredients

4 eggs
1 oz butter
2 tbsp cream (or milk)

Salt and black pepper
Parsley chopped fine (optional)

Method

Beat the eggs lightly, as for an omelette, season them, add the cream. Melt the butter in a saucepan and pour in the mixture and stir over a moderate heat until the eggs begin to set. Take off heat at once - the mixture must never get pebbly. Place on crustless toast, if you like toast, and sprinkle the parsley on top. If not, serve with brown bread.

For scrambled egg, as for an omelette, the grateful recipient should be seated, waiting eagerly.

Buttered Eggs _____

I prefer this to scrambled egg. The flavour of the butter is quite discernible and the mixture lighter. I remember having flu very badly when I was a girl and being unable to eat, until my mother tempted me with this. She cooked it in an earthenware jar in the oven.

Ingredients

2 eggs
1 oz butter

Salt and pepper to taste

Method

Melt the butter, barely, it must not get hot. Break the eggs into a bowl and beat lightly as for an omelette, seasoning to taste. Pour into the saucepan and stir over a moderate heat until egg thickens. Serve on toast, or with brown bread.

Danish Eggs _____

This I learnt from my Swedish friend, Evelyn Jansson, when she lived in Ireland. As well as serving as an hors d'oeuvre, Danish eggs, with the addition of brown bread and a green salad, make a substantial and tasty cold lunch. They are also a good dish for a party.

Ingredients

6 hard-boiled eggs, shelled
    under running cold water and
    halved
4 heaped tbsp mayonnaise,
    home-made
3 - 4 tbsp whipped cream

1 large, hard, eating apple
1 large skinned tomato
1 tsp mild curry powder
Salt and white pepper to taste

Method

Peel and dice the apple. De-seed the tomato and dice. Mix the mayonnaise and the whipped cream together, add the curry powder, salt and pepper to taste. Now mix in the apple and tomato and finally smother the eggs, cut in half, in this delicious mixture. Leave for several, at least two, hours for the curry to impregnate everything else.

Cheese Soufflé _____

Ingredients

4 oz cheddar cheese, grated
1 oz butter
1 oz flour
2 eggs

1 extra egg white
$1/4$ pint milk
$1/2$ tsp salt and black pepper
Dash of cayenne pepper

Method

Pre-heat oven to 400F, 200C, gas 6. Separate the eggs, beat the egg yolk lightly and whisk the whites until stiff. Melt the butter and add the flour. Take saucepan off heat, stir in some of the milk until smooth and return to heat, add the rest of the milk gradually and cook over gentle heat for 3 or 4 minutes, until mixture is smooth and thick. Take off heat again, add the cheese, the egg yolks and the seasoning. Beat until smooth. Fold in the egg whites with a metal spoon. Have ready a greased soufflé dish about 6" in diameter and 3" deep with the usual band of paper tied around the edge, projecting $1^1/_2$" - 2 " above rim of dish. Turn soufflé mixture in and bake for 35 - 40 minutes. Eat at once.

Florentine Eggs _____

Florentine eggs are just baked eggs bedded down in spinach. If you like spinach you will find the combination good. If you detest it, as so many curiously seem to do, then the eggs will not be any compensation.

Ingredients

4 eggs
12 oz freshly cooked spinach to
  which you add:
A pinch of nutmeg in the
  cooking
(Frozen spinach will do
  although it does not taste quite
  as good)

$^1/_2$ oz butter
Salt and black pepper to taste

Method

Pre-heat oven to 350F, 180C, gas 5. Grease 4 ramekin dishes (small oven-proof bowls will do) with the butter. Make sure the spinach is a purée, not a liquid mess. Divide the spinach equally among the ramekins. Slide an egg on top of each. Season with salt, pepper and a suspicion of nutmeg. Cook for 7 to 15 minutes, depending on how well-done you like your eggs.

Egg Mousse

Ingredients

4 hard-boiled eggs
1 tbsp grated cheese, Parmesan
 or cheddar
$1/2$ pint aspic (packet will do)

$1/2$ tsp lime pickle or a dash of
 tabasco sauce
Salt and black pepper to taste

Method

Separate the yolks from the whites of the eggs, chopping the latter finely. Put all ingredients into a bowl and blend thoroughly, or if you have blender, put them all into that and let it do the work. I add the lime pickle to give the necessary lift to the other bland materials, but if preferred, a dash of tabasco sauce will serve this purpose.

Egg mousse looks very pretty with something green garnishing it: courgettes cooked for a few minutes in boiling water and flavoured with lemon, or the more conventional cucumber, or, failing all else, some sprigs of parsley.

Fish

Poached Salmon

Ingredients

A tail-end piece of wild salmon

A *court bouillon* for which
will be needed:
1 carrot
1 onion
1 celery stalk
1 sprig of parsley
1 bay leaf
2 peppercorns

Method

Make the *court bouillon* by putting the vegetables and herbs into enough water to cover salmon. Bring to the boil and simmer for 10 minutes.

Take off water and slide in salmon. Bring back to simmer and immediately lower heat to the point where only an occasional bubble breaks the surface. This is most important, and if your heat cannot be controlled to this point, grill, fry or bake your salmon. Poach for 20 minutes to the lb. If the salmon is to be eaten cold, leave it in the liquid until required. If hot take out and remove skin.

My mother held that salt should never be added in the cooking of fish and I have always followed her advice. Serve with home-made mayonnaise.

A dry German wine, such as Riesling or a Sylvaner is good with this.

Steamed Mackerel _____

Ingredients

2 medium-sized mackerel as
  fresh as possible
2 sprigs of parsley

2 oz butter
Black pepper

Method

Have ready pot of boiling water. Open each mackerel and put
a good sprig of parsley, 1 oz of butter and a dash of pepper
along the inside. Close up and place in steamer. Put steamer
on pot of boiling water and cover tightly. The mackerel will
take from 10 to 15 minutes to cook.

Meantime make a béchamel sauce (page 92) with chopped
up parsley and fennel - the feathery green tops of the bulb -
added.

Plain boiled (if new) or steamed potatoes should be served
with this dish. If your mackerel are fresh enough, it will be
delectable.

Mackerel may, of course, be grilled with mustard (made-
up) spread on the unskinned side. It is good this way too, but
not so delectable.

Herrings in Guinness _____

I hate fish wrapped in what I call 'swaddling clothes' - dipped
in flour. If you get the temperature of the oil right, it needs no
such protection.

Ingredients

4 herrings
4 sprigs of parsley

4 sprigs of fennel
$1/4$ pint of Guinness

Method

Heat enough grape-seed oil, with knob of butter, to cover bottom of frying pan. Put a sprig of parsley and fennel in each herring and slide them into the hot oil. Cook for a few minutes. Pour the Guinness into tilted pan and continue cooking for another few minutes when the herrings will be ready.

This is unexpectedly good, and is the result of my having some Guinness left over from another operation.

Smoked Haddock with Cheese and Cream

Very filling, a favourite Friday dish when I was a child. The best smoked haddock is from Scotland.

Ingredients

$3/4$ lb to 1 lb of Finnan haddock
2 oz grated Cheshire cheese
$1/4$ pint cream

Parsley finely chopped
Black pepper

Method

Put haddock into pan with cold water to cover and bring to the boil. Discard water and rinse pan. Put back on heat, add haddock and cream and bring to simmering for 5 minutes. Sprinkle over the grated cheese with dash of pepper. Continue cooking until the cheese has dissolved and forms a thick sauce. The time will vary with the thickness of the fish which should be divided into 3 or 4 pieces for even cooking.

Serve at once with the parsley sprinkled over, and with cucumber lightly cooked in the minimum of water and flavoured with lemon-juice.

Tuna with Leeks and Potatoes

Ingredients

1 tin of tuna	1 packet leek soup
4 leeks	$1/2$ pink of milk
6 potatoes	Parsley chopped
2 ozs grated cheddar cheese	White pepper

Method

Pre-heat oven to 375F, 190C, gas 5. Peel and slice potatoes. Wash and cut leeks into 1 inch pieces. Turn out tuna and flake. Layer vegetables and tuna in an enamel gratin dish. Make up the leek soup with the $1/2$ pint of milk and pour over the ingredients in the dish. Sprinkle pepper, parsley and cheese on top. Place in oven and bake for 45 - 50 minutes.

One could, if one had the time, make a béchamel sauce instead of the packet soup but it is quite good as it is.

A robust white wine, Spanish perhaps, goes with this.

Salmon-Trout

I once spent another short holiday before term began with my Swedish friend, Evelyn Jansson, in a cottage on the coast near Arklow. One night it blew a ferocious equinoctial storm and the next morning the little river nearby was stiff with dead salmon-trout. The wind had blown the sand up the river and choked the fish. The local people were afraid to touch them. Apparently there was a superstition that anything that came free to one was dangerous! Evelyn Jansson, however, had been brought up in Helsingborg and was an expert on fish. She cut the throat of one of the salmon-trout and knew by the colour of the blood that all was well. We had salmon-trout that week in every shape and form, hot, tepid and cold. We whipped up mayonnaise at the tinkle of a fork, and what's more, I discovered a colony of mushrooms free for the picking. One morning, not being able to agree in what direction to take a walk, she went one way and I another. I was walking through bracken when suddenly I smelt mushrooms. I came on a large patch of a kind I did not recognise, they were taller and bigger and whiter than the usual field mushrooms. I had to fetch the Swede, also an expert on mushrooms. She pronounced them edible and said they were called the "tall proud ones" in Swedish but did not know their name in English. I went one even better than this. The next day I discovered some chanterelles, so to the delicious salmon-trout were now added the extra delights of mushrooms, freshly picked every day. It was an unrehearsed gourmet week. I should add that our local friends, when they saw that we were unharmed, were emboldened also to enjoy the good food to hand.

Ingredients

3 lb salmon-trout	Parsley, feathery fennel tops or
2 oz butter	dill
1 tbsp lemon juice	Black pepper

Method

I think salmon-trout, the most delicious fish of all, is perhaps better baked than poached. It is such a delicately flavoured fish that a bubble too much of the water might diminish some of the flavours. If you have the kind of enamel dish with cover mentioned already and it is big enough to take the length of the fish, use this. If not, wrap up well in foil. Pre-heat oven to 350F, 180C, gas 4. Put half the butter with the herbs, half the lemon juice and a dash of pepper in the inside of the fish. Smooth the rest of the butter over the fish with another dash of pepper and the remaining lemon. Put into enamel dish or, foil-wrapped, into an ordinary baking tin. Cook for about 1 hour. Open and serve with baking juices poured over.

Offer a Chablis with salmon-trout or salmon for a special occasion.

Cods' Tongues _____

Ingredients

I once got a present of Cods' tongues from Newfoundland. I poached them in a *court bouillon*, let them cool and served them in mayonnaise. They were delicious, "melting moments", as we used to say when we were children. But it is a case of first catch your hare. I have never seen them for sale in Ireland.

Poultry and Game

Roast Chicken with Roast Potatoes ___

I have cooked chicken this way over a turf fire using my iron pot. It is equally good but slightly different in taste, which shows that the kind of heat, the sort of utensil, everything, affects the flavour of the food.

Ingredients

3 lb chicken
$1/2$ orange divided into six portions
$1/2$ onion chopped

1 tsp each dried thyme, ground coriander, salt and black pepper
Grape-seed oil and knob of butter

Method

Pre-heat oven to 450F, 220C, gas 8. Use a covered enamel dish. Heat grape-seed oil with an added knob of butter to cover bottom of dish. Mix thyme, coriander, salt and pepper together. Cut orange into six portions, chop the onion. Remove any fatty lumps from bird and wipe over with kitchen paper. Insert first half the pieces of orange, next the onion and then the rest of the orange into body of bird. Sprinkle the mixture of seasoning and herbs over the chicken.

When the oil is sizzling hot, put the chicken in and cover. Place in oven and cook for 20 minutes. Meantime peel and wash 4 good sized potatoes, dry and salt them. After 20 minutes take dish from oven, baste chicken and place potatoes around it. Return to oven and cook for another 20 minutes. Take dish out again, turn chicken and potatoes over. Reduce heat to 350F, 180C, gas 4 and continue to cook for another 20 minutes at least, perhaps a little more if a leg of the bird when wriggled around does not move easily. Turn off the heat and leave to settle for a while (about 10 minutes) before serving.

This method never fails to produce a tender, golden, flavoursome bird. Discard onions but serve the orange portions. Some people, of course, are addicted to the usual bread stuffing. The chicken will take a little longer to cook if this is used.

Serve a dry white wine such as a Verdicchio, or a claret.

Coq au Vin

The whiskey in this recipe is optional but there is nothing that alcohol fails to improve except the human conscience. If you have only brandy in the house, that may of course be used!

Ingredients

3 lb chicken
2 lb mushrooms
1 onion thinly sliced
2 oz butter

1 clove of garlic finely chopped
1 can of red wine sauce
1 tbsp of whiskey (optional)
Salt and black pepper to taste

Method

Pre-heat oven to 350F, 180C, gas 4. Heat grape-seed oil with 1 oz butter in casserole and brown chicken all over. Warm the whiskey, put a match to it and pour the flaming liquor over the chicken. When the flames subside, pour the warmed sauce over.

Meantime cook the onions in a frying pan until transparent. Add the sliced mushrooms and cook for a few minutes. Add to chicken casserole with the garlic, pepper and salt. Cover casserole, place in oven and cook for $1^1/_4$ to $1^1/_2$ hours. Taste for tenderness.

Steamed Chicken _____

My first steamed chicken was the result of straightened circumstances, so to speak. I was on the island of Achill, County Mayo, one summer in a rented house of which the kitchen equipment left a lot to be desired. Neither was it possible to buy raw material on the impulse. A young mountainy butcher came down once a week with the most delicious lamb I have ever tasted, no doubt the result of the animals feeding on some mountain herbs, and a travelling van from Westport came also once a week with baby beef, in its own way equally delicious.

A day or two before either was due, I met unexpectedly some English friends of friends who had to be entertained. What was I to do? I was lucky; I found a source of young chickens. The next problem to be solved was how to cook them. I had no grill and they were too young to be roasted, too tender to be boiled. Suddenly the solution came to me - steam them. But when I rummaged around in the kitchen, I discovered there was no steamer. Then my eye fell on a colander. And that is how I steamed my chickens, one at a time, in the colander over a pot of boiling water with the lid on top.

Ingredients

3 lb chicken
1/2 lemon or 1/4 grapefruit

1/2 onion
Salt and black pepper to taste

Method

Set water in saucepan to boil. Cut lemon or grapefruit into six pieces; chop onion fine. Wipe the chicken and remove any lumps of fat. Fill chicken first with half the fruit, all the onion and then the rest of the fruit. Season to taste. Place chicken in steamer over boiling water. Cover tightly and cook for about 1 1/2 hours. Make sure that the heat is enough to keep water at boiling point but check that it does not boil away. If serving cold, leave to cool over water.

Steamed chicken, the skin removed, is delicious hot served with a parsley white sauce (page 92) to which a little lemon juice has been added, or it can be eaten cold with home-made mayonnaise. It can also be re-heated in a parsley sauce, or made into chicken salad (see below).

Steamed Chicken Salad _____

A very useful dish if unexpected guests turn up on a Monday for lunch.

Ingredients

Whole steamed chicken, skinned and cut into small pieces, or remains, if that is all you have

Peas cooked and cooled (use frozen peas)

Tomatoes, skinned and cut up

Celery cut very fine

Parsley cut fine

Black olives pitted

Hard-boiled eggs (optional)

Rice boiled in chicken stock and cooled

Oil and vinegar dressing

Amount of vegetables and rice will vary according to the amount of chicken used. So will the amount of the dressing.

Method

Mix the chicken, the vegetables and the rice well together. Pour on dressing which should be enough to coat everything well but not reduce material to mushiness. Gently turn everything over and over. Remove to serving dish and build up into shape of your liking, oblong or pyramid. Decorate dish with parsley sprigs, cucumber slices, quartered tomatoes, black olives etc.

A beautiful dish to look at - and quite delicious. A fresh Spanish or Portuguese white wine is good with this.

Sweet and Sour Chicken _____

Ingredients

3 lb chicken cut into 8 serving portions, or use 8 chicken breasts
3 cloves of garlic
2 oz black olives pitted
2 oz dried apricots
2 oz dried figs
2 tbsp brown sugar, demerara or Muscovado

3 tbsp red wine vinegar
2 tbsp red wine, or orange juice
1 tsp dried thyme, ground cumin, ground ginger
Grated rind of an orange
Some sprigs of parsley and of fresh thyme
3 tbsp grape-seed oil or olive oil.

Method

Mix the spices, herbs and fruit, rind of orange, pepper and salt, oil and vinegar together. Add chicken and leave to marinate overnight. Next day pre-set oven to 350F, 180C or gas 4. Transfer chicken and marinade to casserole. Combine sugar with wine. Pour over chicken and cook, covered, for 20 minutes. Uncover and cook for further 40 to 50 minutes, basting from time to time until chicken is tender.

Serve with orange slices if wished or with tinned mandarin sections. Serve the pan juices separately, or serve the whole from the casserole as it comes from the oven. One can leave the cover on during the whole cooking time but it will take a little longer.

Hasty Risotto

The classic Italian risotto takes a long time to cook, involving as it does, the frying of onions and rice to begin with. I have devised a modified risotto which is well thought of. Here it is:

Ingredients

Stock made from a chicken carcass, a stick or two of celery, a couple of carrots and of onions, all cut up finely, a couple of sprigs of parsley and a bay leaf. Let this simmer for at least 15 minutes after it has come to the boil
$2^1/_2$ cups stock will be needed

1 cup rice
1 tomato
The remains of the chicken
A few scraps of bacon, if you have it
Salt and pepper

Method

Measure the stock into a saucepan through a sieve. Add the rice, salt and pepper. Bring to the boil, stir, reduce to a gentle simmer and cook, stirring once or twice more, for 20 minutes. Add the diced chicken and tomato and cook for another 15 minutes. If the rice dries too quickly, add a little more stock and continue cooking until all the liquid is absorbed. At this stage, you must watch your risotto carefully to make sure it does not stick to the saucepan.

Serve with various chutneys - mango, peach, lime etc.

Turkey Breasts in Cream and Lemon Juice

Ingredients

8 oz of turkey breast
$1/4$ pint cream
$1^1/_2$ tbsp lemon juice

Salt and black pepper
$1^1/_2$ tbsp flour

Method

Heat 2 tbsp grape-seed oil and a knob of butter in a large saucepan with lid. Cut the turkey breast in two if it is in one piece. Dip in cream, just enough to cover, then in seasoned flour. Have heat fairly high. Put turkey in, seal for two minutes on both sides, lower heat, cover pan and continue cooking for 15 to 20 minutes in all depending on thickness of turkey pieces. Just before they are ready, push to one side, tilt pan, pour in remainder of cream, raise heat and amalgamate oil and cream. Then add lemon juice and mix this well in. Serve turkey breasts covered in the creamy sauce. Rice goes well with this dish, as does steamed fennel and tomatoes. But mushrooms do equally well.

The wine to offer is a Sylvaner.

Pheasant _____

Ingredients

1 pheasant	1 handful parsley
4 oz butter	Salt and black pepper to taste

Method

Pre-heat oven to 450F, 220C, gas 8. Divide butter into two portions. Wipe out bird and stuff with half the butter and the well-washed parsley. Smooth the rest of the butter over the breast. Heat the grape-seed oil in enamel baking dish. Put bird in dish, cover and cook at high heat for 20 minutes. Take out and baste. Lower heat to 375F, 190C, gas 5 and continue cooking for another 40 minutes. Serve with celery and bread sauce, discard parsley.

Mrs Beeton suggests putting $1/4$ lb of beef in the inside of the pheasant. I have never tried this but the experimentalists among my readers might.

A pheasant may be cooked in a casserole. If this is required, marinate overnight in marinade for *Boeuf en Daube*, substituting rosemary for the bay leaf.

Duck

Ingredients

4 lb duck
$1/2$ bottle red wine
Salt, pepper and ground
   coriander to taste

Stuffing as for Pork Steaks,
   substituting a little sage, finely
   chopped, for thyme

Method

Pre-heat oven to 450F, 320C, gas 8. Prick skin of duck all over. Stuff and season. Heat just enough grape-seed oil to cover bottom of enamel baking dish. Put rack in dish and place duck on it. Cover and cook at high heat for 30 minutes. Take out and pour off fat. Gently heat wine. Put duck back in dish and pour wine around (not over). Reduce heat to 375F, 190C, gas 5. Continue cooking for another hour.

The wine and remaining fat from duck will form a delicious jelly when cold.

Roast Quail

I spent a Christmas once in Venice, the guest of Darina Silone, Ignazio Silone's widow, and an old friend from University College Dublin. I developed a passion for quail, though I felt like a self-indulgent savage as I ate them.

Ingredients

4 quail
4 streaky rashers
2 ozs butter

4 sprigs parsley
Black pepper

Method

Pre-heat oven to 425F, 220C, gas 7. Put sprig of parsley and $1/2$ oz of butter in each quail. Shake over a little pepper and wrap a rasher round each little bird. Have your oil hot in pan, put in quails and roast for 10 to 15 minutes.

Mustardy Rabbit _____

Ingredients

1 rabbit
1 jar of strong Dijon mustard
$^1/_4$ pint of cream

2 oz butter
1 glass of dry white wine
Salt, pepper, and a little grape-
  seed oil.

Method

Pre-heat oven to 425F, 220C, gas 7. Rub the rabbit with the oil, salt and pepper, cover all over with a thick layer of mustard, dot with the butter and place in the heated oven. Cook for 30 minutes, then pour the wine over the rabbit and return to the oven for another 15 minutes. Remove rabbit to serving dish and disjoint it. Keep warm while you add cream to the other juices in the cooking pan and amalgamate well. Pour this rich sauce over your rabbit and eat the delicious result.

This recipe comes from Mrs Margaret O'Keefe of Coleraine, and is the happy result of a recent academic occasion there. The pleasures of an External Examiner are unexpectedly enhanced in such ways.

Meat

Frying and Grilling _____

I have an Italian friend who lived for many years in Ireland. She used to say that she thoroughly approved of the Irish method of cooking - ten minutes in the kitchen with a frying pan.

Now, there is no denying that the quickest method of preparing a meal is to fry or grill the meat. The best cuts of meat must be used, well seasoned with herbs and spices - cinnamon or coriander for lamb, powdered bay leaves for beef, garlic for both. For frying use as little oil as possible. I use grape-seed oil with a knob of butter added. If grilling, smear the meat and the rack with oil. Better still marinate in a little oil and lemon juice. Use a high heat for the first few minutes to sear the meat and then lower to cook gently through for another few minutes.

The vegetables can be put to steam simultaneously and garlicky potatoes likewise made. Half-an-hour is all the time required. Once the searing has been done, I cover the pan to keep in the juicy moisture. If the skin is still left on the meat, remove it and any thick fat, but leave some fat - it adds to the flavour, and some fat is necessary for healthy eating.

To Cook a Ham

This dish may be prepared in three stages: steeping overnight; cooking in *court bouillon*; and the oven-glazing the following day. Traditionally a Christmas dish, but useful at any time as a standby; the bone can be used to make flavoursome stock for a risotto.

Ingredients

1 ham or large piece of gammon
2 carrots
1 onion
1 stick of celery
4 peppercorns
$1/2$ cup demerara sugar

$1/2$ pint cider, or cider vinegar
1 bay leaf
1 garlic clove
Sprig of parsley
Sprig of thyme

Method

Steep overnight in cold water. Scrape skin before putting back into cold water and bring slowly to boil. Meantime prepare a *court bouillon* by boiling the sliced carrots, onion, celery, garlic clove, peppercorns, parsley, thyme and demerara sugar in water. When ham has come to the boil, empty water, rinse saucepan, pour *court bouillon* and cider over the ham and bring back to the boil. Reduce heat to simmer and cook slowly for 25 minutes to the lb.

At this point the ham can be left overnight, if convenient, in the cooking liquid, or it may be finished straight away.

Heat oven to 425F, 220C, gas 7 and mix the following *glaze*:

2 level tbsp of mustard powder,
2 level tbsp of whiskey
4 tbsp of honey

Amalgamate the ingredients well and pour over the ham which has been placed in a roasting tin. Cook for 15 - 20 minutes if ham is still warm, for longer if it is cold, until the glaze has turned golden.

Like all joints, ham is the better for being left to rest for a while before carving.

Bacon Stew

A succulent, warming dish which I invented and which has risen on my scale of values since it successfully served as a test of my cooking, on an important occasion, when I had two high-powered ladies to dinner!

Ingredients

1³/₄ to 2 lb piece of streaky bacon
4 medium-sized potatoes
4 medium-sized onions
4 carrots
4 sticks of celery
1 orange
1 hard apple

4 sprigs of parsley
4 sprigs of thyme
2 tsps of medium or mild curry powder, according to taste; if preferred, mustard powder may be substituted
Salt and freshly ground black pepper

Method

Put bacon in cold water and bring to the boil. Meantime prepare vegetables - peel and quarter potatoes, halve onions. Cut celery and carrots into half-inch pieces, cut unpeeled orange into quarters, core and halve unpeeled apple.

When the bacon has come to the boil, discard water and rinse. Put trivet in bottom of pressure cooker. Place potatoes over it, season lightly. Put bacon on top and cover with vegetables and fruit, seasoning again. Add parsley and thyme. Mix curry powder with a teaspoon or two of warm water and add this to the quantity of water necessary to cover the contents of the pressure cooker. Pour the water over the bacon and vegetables. Put on lid and bring to pressure. Reduce heat to sustain correct pressure. Cook for half an hour.

Serve it with a palatable *vin de table*, such as a *Prestige du Patron*.

Plain Boiled Bacon and Cabbage _____

Traditionally in Ireland boiled bacon was served with cabbage done in the same water but I think a much better plan is to cook the potatoes with the bacon and do the cabbage separately.

For this, pre-boil the bacon as in the method described above. Put bacon back into saucepan with cold water to cover and a carrot, an onion, parsley and thyme for flavouring. Bring to boil, and then simmer for 25 minutes to the lb. and 25 minutes over. An hour before the end of cooking time, add the well-scrubbed but unpeeled potatoes to the pot; bring back to boil and reduce to simmer once again.

Serve with a parsley white sauce (page 92).

Bacon
another method _____

Pre-boil the bacon joint; place it in a tight-fitting saucepan and pour over half a bottle of Guinness. Fill up with cold water and bring slowly to the boil. Let simmer for five minutes only.

Allow to cool in the liquor, overnight if you wish. Then take out, stud it with a few cloves and rub in a little demerara sugar or honey and some mustard. Wrap in foil and bake in oven at 350F, 180C, gas 4 for twenty-five minutes to the lb.

If one has time to spare the night before serving, the preliminary cooking can be done then, and there is little to do on the day but pop it into the oven.

Stuffed Pork Steaks _____

Kate O'Brien, invited to lunch once by my mother, and served such pork steaks said she had thought it was only in Limerick you got them. Always serve pork steaks with apple sauce.

Ingredients

2 pork steaks
$1/_2$ lb fine breadcrumbs
2 oz butter
1 onion
2 sprigs of parsley chopped
2 sprigs of thyme, chopped

1 onion, or one clove of garlic
  crushed
$1/_2$ pint of milk
1 tbsp whiskey (optional)
Salt and black pepper

Method

Pre-heat oven to 375F, 190C, gas 5. Cut pork steaks down the middle but not all the way through. Lay out flat and remove any membrane or fat. Chop the onion fine and put into milk; bring to the boil and leave to infuse. Mix the breadcrumbs, herbs, chopped-up butter, salt and pepper in a bowl. Take out onion from milk and add to breadcrumb mixture, making sure it is very finely chopped. Gradually add milk enough to produce a well-moistened but solid mixture; finally add the whiskey, if using. My advice would be not to overlook the whiskey; it enhances all stuffing. Halve the stuffing and lay along the pork steaks. Roll up from narrower end and either skewer or tie up with strong thread.

When I was a child the crusts of bread left over from making the crumbs used to be put at either end of the pork parcels before tying, but a square of foil, dull side in, does equally well. Have enough grape-seed oil heated in pan and put pork steaks in and cook for 45 minutes. Be sure not to overcook. If your oven is fast, lower heat.

My mother used to serve braised parsnips with this dish but I never liked parsnips and serve instead a green vegetable, peas, buttered leeks, celery with lemon juice, etc.

This dish is equally good hot or cold.

Whiskey in the stuffing was not invented by me but by my

sister, Mabel FitzGerald Smith, who once found herself confronted by a turkey that had been more than adequately hung. It was too late to go looking for another turkey, so she set to and first rubbed her odorous bird well with vinegar then with liberal applications of whiskey, finally using whiskey to moisten her bread stuffing. To make assurance doubly sure, she added a little to the sausage meat intended for the craw. This is now handed down in the legends of her family as the best turkey ever.

A claret is good with pork: *Château de Jau* for special occasions.

Breaded Pork Chops

Ingredients

4 centreloin pork chops
4 oz breadcrumbs, fairly fresh
1 egg beaten and seasoned

1 clove of garlic
1 sprig of rosemary finely chopped or 1 tsp of dried rosemary

Method

Insert sliver of garlic clove between meat and fat of each chop. Beat egg and season to taste with salt and black pepper. Add rosemary. Dip each chop into beaten egg and then immediately cover with breadcrumbs. Have grape-seed oil and knob of butter heated in heavy-bottomed frying pan. Put chops in and cook on high heat for 2 minutes on each side. Lower heat and continue cooking for another five minutes on each side. Some people season the breadcrumbs instead of the egg, but I prefer to keep the seasoning as near the meat as possible. A tender, moist dish but rich, not for everyday.

Offer a dry cider, perhaps, with this.

Cannelloni _____

Ingredients

8 pancakes (page 135)

For the stuffing:
1 lb of minced beef
$^1/_2$ lb cooked ham
2 oz Parmesan cheese
Béchamel sauce

Method

First make the pancakes (page 135).

Pre-heat oven to 375F, 190C, gas 5. Cook the minced beef, lean not fatty beef, in grape-seed oil. Add the ham and the grated Parmesan. Spread an equal quantity on each pancake. Fold up and place in baking tin. Pour béchamel sauce over the pancakes and cook for 25 minutes until golden and bubbling.

Ideally, offer a Frascati with this, but any light dry white wine will serve.

Moussaka

Ingredients

2¹/₂ lbs medium-sized
  aubergines
1 medium-sized onion, chopped
1¹/₂ lbs minced meat (lean)
3 skinned and chopped tomatoes
2 oz butter
¹/₄ pint white wine

2 oz toasted breadcrumbs
3 eggs
³/₄ pint béchamel sauce
4 oz cheddar cheese grated
Parsley chopped
Salt and black pepper

Method

Pre-heat oven to 375F, 180C, gas 5. Cut aubergines into slices
¹/₂" thick. Sprinkle with salt and leave for one hour. Sauté the
onion until soft. Add minced meat and 4 tbsp of water. Cook,
stirring constantly to break up the meat. Add the wine,
tomatoes, parsley and pepper and simmer covered for 45
minutes. Remove from fire. Beat up two of the egg whites
separated from the yolks, add these and the breadcrumbs to the
mixture and stir well.

Rinse the salt from the aubergines and dry well. Fry them
lightly in olive oil on both sides.

Have ready a greased oven proof dish 9" x 13", sprinkle the
bottom with breadcrumbs and cover with half the aubergine
slices. Now add the meat and tomato mixture and cover with
the remaining aubergine slices. Beat the egg yolks with the
remaining whole egg and mix with the béchamel sauce. Add
most of the grated cheese and pour over the ingredients
already in the dish. Sprinkle over the rest of the cheese and
bake for about 45 minutes, until the top is golden brown.

Moussaka is made in Greece also with other vegetables,
such as potatoes and courgettes, but the only one I like
confines itself to aubergines. A can of tomatoes may be used,
if more convenient, instead of the fresh tomatoes. The
quantities given here may be halved, of course, but the large
dish will serve up to 8 people, and is useful for a party. The
meat mixture, with the substitution of red wine for white, can
be used for *lasagna* and *spaghetti bolognese*.

Roast Beef and Yorkshire Pudding _____

Kate O'Brien once told a waiter in the Shelbourne Hotel, Dublin, that the Chef, or commis chef as the case might be, should take a lesson from my mother in the cooking of Yorkshire Pudding. Of course, if one cannot spare the time to make the Yorkshire Pudding, the roast beef remains delicious in itself. I learnt once from a farmer that the best beef came from a Hereford animal, while the Friesian was the best for milking.

Ingredients

3 lbs of sirloin of beef on the bone
1 clove of garlic
1 tbsp each of seasoned flour and mustard powder

For the Yorkshire Pudding:
3 tbsp of sifted flour
1 egg
1 tsp salt and dust of black pepper
Milk, or water, as required.

Method

Pre-heat oven to 425F, 220C, gas 7. Make incisions between bone and meat and insert tiny slices of garlic. Mix flour and mustard powder together, rub this over the surface of the joint. Place in a well-oiled baking tin and cook for 15 minutes. Lower heat to 350F, 180C, gas 4 and continue cooking for 15 minutes to the lb and 15 minutes over for rare meat, 20 minutes to the lb for well-done. Half-way through, baste and turn joint.

To make the *Yorkshire Pudding,* sift flour and salt into bowl. Make hole in middle and break egg into it. Beat well until all is amalgamated. Add milk or water until a stiff pouring consistency is reached and all is smooth and bubbly. Leave in a cool place for at least half an hour then beat again. 15 to 20 minutes before end of cooking time, remove the joint from the oven and take it out of the tin. Pour batter into tin and replace joint. Put back in the oven for the remaining 15 or 20 minutes.

Done this way, the juices from the meat soak into the batter and a luscious, gooey confection results. A far cry indeed from the little dried rounds of so-called Yorkshire Pudding often served in hotels.

Offer a Burgundy or Rhône wine.

Goulash

Ingredients

1¹/₂ lbs of round beef
6 medium-sized onions, sliced
2 cloves of garlic
1 heaped tbsp of paprika

1 tsp of caraway seeds
¹/₂ pint of beef stock (a good beef cube will do) if possible; if not use water, salt and black pepper to taste.

Method

Cut the beef into 2 inch-sized pieces. Heat enough grape-seed oil to fry the onions until they are transparent. Push to one side and sear the meat quickly. Transfer meat and onions to pressure cooker. Add paprika, sliced garlic gloves, caraway seeds, salt and pepper. Warm the beef stock if you have it, if not use water, and add it to the pot. Bring to pressure. Reduce heat to maintain pressure. Cook for 15 minutes.

A fragrant warming dish which we call Hungarian Goulash but which is not found in Hungary where Goulash is a soup. Serve mushrooms done in garlic and butter with this, and rice or new potatoes.

A claret goes well with this dish.

Ordinary Beef Stew _____

Some people think a stew is not a stew without carrots, so serve them this and keep the Goulash for gourmets.

To make an ordinary beef stew, omit paprika and substitute a couple of bay leaves or powdered bay leaves. Add some carrots - about 4 medium-sized ones sliced. Dip the beef in seasoned flour before serving and then proceed as for Goulash above.

Boeuf en Daube _____

I don't remember where I got this recipe, but it was a great success the first time I served it - after Christmas when everybody was sick and tired of turkey and all its works and pomps. It has been a great standby ever since.

Ingredients

2 lbs of round beef
3 onions finely sliced
$1/2$ bottle of rough red wine
$1/4$ pint of olive oil

1 tsp powdered bay leaf
1 tsp dried thyme
2 lbs of mashed potatoes
Salt and black pepper to taste

Method

Mix the wine, oil, thyme and powdered bay leaf. Put the beef and onions to marinate overnight in mixture.

Next day take out beef, cut into 2 inch-sized pieces. Dry and brown in olive oil. Remove to casserole. Add salt and pepper and the marinade. Cover with the mashed potatoes. Put into oven 325F, 170C, gas 3 and cook for 2 hours until beef is tender.

Some of the potatoes will melt into the liquid making a delicious thick gravy. If more potatoes are needed, serve some cooked separately. Accompany with a green salad.

Like all casseroles, this reheats well in gentle heat although one must be sure to reheat very thoroughly.

Tongue
cooked in pressure cooker _____

Tongue was a favourite dish of mine when I was a child - maybe because it was so easy to swallow. I had what people of the time called 'a narrow swallow' or a 'small swallow'. I think myself it was simply that I choked over food a lot because, while I liked eating, I hated chewing. My dear friend, the late Dudley Edwards, said to me shortly before he died: "Lorna, you eat too fast, it is very bad for you." To which I replied - "So people have been telling me all my life, Dudley, but here I am, still to the good."

Ingredients

1 ox tongue, about 4 lbs
1 onion, carrot, stick of celery
Bay leaf
2 sprigs of parsley and of thyme

2 cloves
12 peppercorns
2 tbsp vinegar (wine or cider)

Method

Wash tongue and if it has been pickled, soak for several hours. Remove trivet from pot, put in all ingredients, with water to half fill pressure cooker. Bring to pressure and cook for 15 minutes to the lb at high pressure. Allow pressure to reduce at room temperature.

Take out tongue, skin carefully and remove the small bones and any fatty bits at root end. If serving hot, put back into liquid to keep warm while you make a parsley sauce.

If you want the tongue cold, roll up and put into an 8" or 9" pudding bowl. Pour some of the cooking liquid over. Put a weighted plate on top and leave for 24 hours if possible but at least for 12 hours. In the old way a tongue had to simmer for three hours, so the pressure cooker is truly an invaluable invention.

Heavenly Veal _____

This I invented and it is so-called because guests eating it for the first time kept saying "It's heavenly!". But perhaps 'Celestial Veal' would be a better name.

My mother had a dish called 'Enchanted Veal' the recipe for which she acquired in Jamaica, but it is a cold dish and therefore not at all in the same class as a hot one.

Ingredients

1 lb veal escalopes cut into
  pieces
2 onions
1 small or half a large cucumber
6 oz mushrooms
$^{1}/_{2}$ pint cream

$1^{1}/_{2}$ tbsp lemon juice
1 clove of garlic
1 oz butter
Seasoned flour

Method

Pre-heat oven to 375F, 190C, gas 5. The onions, cucumbers and mushrooms must be pre-cooked separately. Boil the sliced cucumber in the minimum of water until transparent. Discard water and reserve. Soften the sliced onions in grape-seed oil and the sliced mushroom in butter with the chopped up garlic. Dip the veal in seasoned flour. Heat enough grape-seed oil to cover bottom of open oblong-shaped enamel gratin dish. Put veal, onions, mushrooms with cooking juices and cucumber in dish. Cover with cream, add lemon juice. Cook for $^{1}/_{2}$ to $^{3}/_{4}$ hour until all constituents are tender and melted into one another. Not a quick dish to prepare but admirable for a special occasion.

Serve a dry white wine - a Blanc de Blancs or a light White Bordeaux.

Saltimbocca

I include this because it brings back memories of a summer I spent in Rome. I used to eat in a little *trattoria* behind Piazza Navona where the food was very good and much cheaper than in the rather grand *ristoranti* on Piazza Navona itself. Many years, almost twelve, later, I was once more in Rome and I went in search of the *Bar Senato*, more than half expecting it either to have disappeared or become unrecognisable. Not at all. It was just its old, rather shabby self. I sat myself down at the very table I used to choose, when out came the son of the house, much stouter, even more amiable, than he had been. He looked at me and said, "Ben ritornata, Signora." After all those years he had remembered and recognised me. Not only that but he went in and brought out his father to greet me and welcome me back. I was given a Sambucco on the house to celebrate my return. I loved Rome. I could have lived there forever.

Ingredients

1 lb escalope of veal
8 oz cooked ham
2 oz butter
8 sage leaves - young and tender

$1/4$ pint of dry white wine or dry vermouth
1 tbsp olive oil or grape-seed oil

Method

Divide veal into 8 portions. Place over each a smaller piece of ham. Put a sage leaf on top again and roll up into a neat package. Skewer together with a cocktail stick, through the top layer only, not piercing through. Heat half the butter and all the oil in a heavy-bottomed frying pan. As soon as the butter foams, put in the meat rolls and cook on all sides until golden brown.

Raise the heat and pour the wine on. It must be hot enough to cause the wine to evaporate. Take out the meat and place on heated dish. Make sauce out of the pan juices, the remaining butter and tablespoonful or so of boiling water. Be sure to scrape the pan well.

Another rich dish. Serve with plain boiled rice and a green salad.

Lamb Casserole
Economical version _____

To cook economically takes more time - long slow cooking is necessary. But there is a challenge in it and flavouring is more than ever important.

Ingredients

4 lamb shanks halved (about 2 lbs in all)
2 chopped onions
8 small potatoes
4 oz frozen peas
1 clove of garlic

8 juniper berries
2 tsp dill
1 tbsp lemon juice
$1/_2$ pint of warm water, or lamb stock if available
Salt and pepper to taste

Method

Heat a mixture of grape-seed and olive oil in flame-proof casserole and brown shanks all over. Remove and add onions, cooking until transparent. Sprinkle in flour and cook for 2 minutes. Gradually blend in stock or water, and return lamb to casserole. Bring to the boil, skimming off any foam that forms. Add juniper berries, garlic sliced, dill, salt and pepper. Cover and simmer very gently for one hour.

Now add potatoes and simmer for another 45 - 50 minutes. Stir in peas and lemon juice and simmer for a further 5 or 10 minutes. This may be cooked in the oven, 350F, 180C, gas 4. But don't forget to add the potatoes and the peas before the end of cooking time.

Serve a light claret or a dry cider.

Roast Loin of Lamb _____

When I got the chair of Modern English in Galway, I moved not to the city, but to the village of Eyrecourt in the country. Among the items that came with the house was an iron pot that seemed like a primitive pressure cooker: it had a valve in the middle of the lid that rose and fell if the contents were cooking too fast. An ancient range - older-seeming than the one in my grandmother's house - had to be scrapped, and I decided to have an open turf fire in its place with a crane for suspending cooking utensils. I discovered that a complete meal could be cooked in the iron pot. When my mother came to stay, she stared aghast at my arrangements and said snootily: "I don't know what you have in mind. It seems to me that you are trying to go back at least two hundred years." She found a sympathetic ear in Evelyn Jansson, who was also staying. I held my peace and pressed ahead with my meal in a pot. When they tasted the food there was a prolonged silence. Then Evelyn spoke up: "Mind you," she said, "that was edible." I heard no more complaints about my backward instincts, and my delight was complete when a friend in the village remarked: "I hear you are going in for antique cooking." All kinds of people, from External Examiners to cousins subsequently enjoyed my antique cooking! My brother-in-law, Harry Fitzgerald Smith, used to say at the same time every year: "I am longing for a bit of lamb from your pot."

Ingredients

Joint of loin made up of 7 to 8 chops
2 cloves of garlic
Large sprigs of rosemary and of parsley
1 tbsp of ground cinnamon
Salt and pepper to taste
Grape-seed oil and olive oil (for roasting)

Method

Pre-heat oven to 450F, 220C, gas 8. Insert slivers of garlic between chops. Fold flap (as much as one gets nowadays) over rosemary and parsley. Skewer to top part. Sprinkle cinnamon all over and rub it into exposed ends.

Heat mixture of grape-seed and olive oil in roasting tin and put in the joint. Cook for 20 minutes at high heat. Lower heat to 350F, 180C, gas 4 and continue cooking for 20 minutes to the lb. and 20 minutes over. Turn the joint half-way through the cooking.

Serve with mint, chopped very finely, mixed with grated peel of a lemon, if wine is offered. If not, serve a classic Mint Sauce (page 95).

This calls for a good wine - a claret, a *Château de Jau*, for instance.

Roast Lamb
Another method _____

Even more delicious, I think, than the classic roast lamb.

Ingredients

Joint of loin made up of 7 to 8
   chops
2 cloves of garlic
Large sprig of rosemary and of
   parsley

1 tbsp of ground cinnamon
Salt and pepper to taste
$1/2$ cup of olive oil
2 tbsp of lemon juice

Method

Pre-heat oven as for *Roast Loin of Lamb*. Marinate the lamb, the garlic slivers inserted, in a well-stirred mixture of olive oil, lemon juice and cinnamon, about $3/4$ cupful, half a measure of lemon juice to one of olive oil. Leave overnight. Cook as for *Roast Loin of Lamb*, reducing heat after first 20 minutes, but allow only 15 minutes per lb and 15 minutes over as the marinade will have tenderised the lamb.

Irish Stew

AE Housman wrote to the Steward of Trinity College Cambridge:

> I am tired of writing in the suggestion book about Irish stew and saying that it ought to have lots of potato and lots of onion. On the last occasion it not only had neither but was strangely and shockingly garnished with dumplings.
> *The Letters of AE Housman* Ed Henry Maas, London, 1971.

The classic Irish stew had just three ingredients, apart from water - potatoes, onions and mutton. I always found it rather insipid. This version of my own I fondly imagine to be greatly improved in flavour. Since mutton seems to have disappeared, I have substituted lamb but it must be 1 year-old and not Spring lamb.

Ingredients

4 gigot lamb chops (not Spring lamb)
4 medium-sized potatoes
4 medium-sized onions
4 white turnips (swedes will not do)

4 cloves of garlic
2 sprigs of parsley
A pinch of dried mint
Salt and black pepper to taste

Method

Peel the potatoes, onions and white turnips. Chop the garlic very fine. Cut the potatoes in 4, the onions in half and the turnips in slices. Cut the meat into 6 portions. Put the potatoes at the bottom of the pressure cooker, add the onions and garlic, then the meat and finally the turnips, seasoning each layer. Add the parsley and sprinkle over a good pinch of dried mint. Pour in $1/2$ pint of warm water. Bring to pressure and cook for 20 minutes. Reduce at room temperature.

Stuffed Shoulder of Lamb _____

Much enjoyed, I am told, in Hong Kong, where one of my sisters lived for many years.

Ingredients

4 lbs boned shoulder of lamb
1 glass of wine vinegar (red or
  white)
$1/_4$ pint of water
1 sprig of rosemary
Few leaves of mint
Bones from the shoulder

For the Stuffing:
$1/_2$ lb sausage meat
2 oz breadcrumbs
1 tsp chives finely chopped
1 tsp parsley and rosemary
  finely chopped
Salt and white pepper to taste
1 clove garlic crushed

Method

Pre-heat oven to 350F, 170C, gas 4. Put the bones into the roasting tin with 2 tbsp grape-seed oil and a dash of salt. Put into pre-heated oven while you make the stuffing. Add all the ingredients for this together, mixing well, the sausage meat going in last. Season. Fork the stuffing into the cavity left by the missing bones. Roll up and tie well. Push the bones in tin to one side, put in lamb and brown for about 20 minutes, turning it at intervals. Mix the wine vinegar and hot water, take out lamb and pour in the vinegar and water. Do not pour it over the joint. Return the lamb to oven sprinkled with chopped rosemary. Cover with foil, tucking it well inside roasting tin. Cook for 2 hours. Serve the juices from the tin as a sauce, adding the chopped mint leaves and 2 tbsp boiling water.

I hate thickened gravies, but for those who like them a little cornflour may be added, boiling everything well for a couple of minutes.

This is good also served cold, with mint jelly or a mild chutney sauce such as apricot.

Vegetables

Never by choice, with one exception, boil vegetables. Steam, bake, or braise them. The exception is **new potatoes** which, for some reason or another, do not steam well. If you do put root vegetables into water, learn to assess just how much water will be sufficient to soften them while being absorbed in the process.

Most green vegetables are best strained, those like **broccoli**, **mangetout peas** and **beans** can be put into a collapsible steamer over a little boiling water and cooked in a few minutes *al dente*, slightly crunchy, never left long enough to become mushy. Tip the vegetables back into the saucepan and add a few drops of lemon juice.

Cabbage, I cook like **spinach**. I shred the cabbage very finely and put it into cold water for half an hour. I melt a nice knob of butter in a heavy-bottomed pan, let it just begin to brown, put the cabbage in with the water adhering to it. Add salt and pepper, cover lightly and cook over high heat for about two minutes, then lower heat for a further four or five minutes until the water is absorbed. Sometimes I add strips of **green pepper** and caraway seeds and sometimes just caraway seeds. The ancient Chinese had a most exalted view of cabbage, and when it is done this way, one understands why.

If I am cooking a **cauliflower** whole, I choose a saucepan into which it will just fit, put two inches of boiling water in the bottom and, in effect, steam it. When I serve it, I often add a tablespoonful or two of mayonnaise, better, I think, than a béchamel sauce.

Courgettes and **cucumber** I slice very finely and put into just enough boiling water to become absorbed when they have reached transparency point after five or six minutes. As I have said already, judging the amount of water necessary is a matter of experience. I put them back into the dry saucepan and add salt and pepper, a knob of butter, and a little lemon juice. **Cucumbers**, done this way, are delicious with fish or pork.

Spinach and **sorrel** are, of course, cooked without water, in butter, with nutmeg added to the spinach and coriander to the sorrel. **Sorrel** constitutes rather a sauce than a vegetable and is delectable with chicken or fish. Uncooked, made into a salad, it is piquant with cold chicken.

Beetroot is much better baked than boiled. Handle it carefully so as not to break the skin. Bake in a moderate oven - 350F, 180C, gas 4 - until the skin is wrinkled. Rub off the skin and slice immediately if it is to be served hot, with melted butter. If cold, leave to cool and then rub off the skin and slice. Serve in a wine-vinegar.

Carrots left plain always seem dull to me, so I add, just when the boiling water is on the point of evaporation, some lemon juice and brown sugar so as to glaze them and create a sweet and sour taste. I do the same thing with **white turnips** to serve with pork. I never cook **swede turnips**. As a child I quite liked them raw but detested them cooked. Some people like a purée of mixed **carrot** and **parsnip**.

Asparagus is a vegetable for the gods. It should be cooked upright in a little boiling water so that the spears are steamed. There is a proper pot for the purpose, but I cook them in an old, narrow, aluminium, hot-water jug.

Celery is another delicious vegetable and believed by the ancient Irish to have potent healing properties. According to the Brehon laws, I am told, any man who maliciously wounded another was obliged to supply him with celery every day until he was cured. To cook it, chop it up very finely, having removed any stringy bits from the side of the stalks, pour on barely enough boiling water to cook the quantity required, cover and cook quickly *al dente* and until the water is absorbed. Add salt and pepper, some lemon juice, reheat and serve at once.

Fennel can be easily found nowadays in the supermarkets. Cut through the bulb, and chop each half finely. Put into collapsible steamer over a little boiling water and cook for about 5 or 6 minutes. Its titillating, aniseedy flavour goes well with chicken, turkey, pork or fish. A purée of fennel and of tomatoes is especially good with turkey. To make the purée you must steam a little longer. The tomatoes can be skinned and steamed with the fennel.

Tomatoes are, perhaps, the most versatile of all vegetables excluding the humble, ubiquitous **potatoes**. They may be fried, steamed, stuffed and baked, eaten raw by themselves or as an ingredient in a salad. The tomato belongs to the same family of plants as the potato, but is a flamboyant relation of its country cousin. It is said to be very rich in Vitamin C. It has the further advantage that it cooks very quickly.

Onions are an indispensable flavouring vegetable, necessary for all stews and essential for *Beef Goulash*. The more delicately flavoured ones, such as Spanish onions, can be used raw in salads. They were frequently served, baked whole, with a joint of mutton, when I was a child, and I still sometimes serve them like this with lamb, as it gets older with the year: they take about 45 minutes to cook.

Onions are said to be good for the heart, the stronger the flavour the better. A horrible, to my taste, concoction used to be made in my grandmother's house for a cold: an onion boiled in milk, flavoured with pepper and nutmeg. Most children detest onions. It is a taste one acquires as one grows older, reassured in the acquisition perhaps, by the remark ascribed by Hardy to one of his characters - 'that he always suspected a man who had no acquired tastes of not being a gentleman.'

Leeks, the gentler relation of the onions, are found palatable even by children. They are best braised, I think. Well-washed and sliced, they are put in an oven-proof dish with a tightly-fitting lid, well-peppered, lightly salted, clotted with butter and cooked for between 30 - 45 minutes at 375F, 190C, gas 5 oven. Leeks are very good with pork or fish, and, cold, can be served in an oil and vinegar dressing as a salad.

Mushrooms can accompany practically anything. I like them done in butter in which a chopped-up clove of garlic has sizzled for a little while. Slice finely, season quickly with salt and pepper. Cover tightly and cook to the desired tenderness, avoiding mushiness. Add a tablespoon or two of dry vermouth, if available, if not, substitute lemon juice. When I was a child, they used to be put on top of the range, sprinkled with salt and pepper and eaten when the juices ran. There was nothing at the time, of course, but wild mushrooms, the more appreciated because their season was so short.

If mushrooms are to be served as an omelette-filler, they are best cooked in cream. For this, omit the garlic but add lemon juice from the start. Cook as above until the mushrooms are nearly done, then mix a dessertspoon of flour and $1/4$ pint of cream well together and pour into the saucepan. Stir well until the mixture boils, then simmer for 10 minutes to cook the flour. Keep warm while you get your omelette going. Add while still somewhat liquidy, fold over and serve. Mushrooms are delicious as a salad (page 86).

Potatoes are still considered indispensable in many Irish homes as part of the main meal of the day. I hated potatoes as a child and consequently found it very difficult to understand why the Great Famine ever happened. Surely there must have been a great many people like me, I thought, who never wanted potatoes - how could so many people have come to rely on them, I wondered. This was when I was still so young that I thought taste alone determined what one ate. But long after the economic and political causes of the Famine had become familiar to me, I still disliked potatoes, and it was not until I ate potatoes grown in Connemara with the use of kelp as manure that I suddenly began to enjoy their taste. 'A new planet had swum into my ken', to misapply my metaphors.

New potatoes are best boiled, put into salted boiling water, but not allowed to boil too quickly, an end best effected by a heavy-bottomed saucepan. Old potatoes, if you want them plain, are best steamed. They can also, of course, be baked in their jackets, just flung into the oven, or peeled, salted, and roasted in the pan with the joint. I do not subscribe to the school that holds they are best roasted separately and I should never dream of first parboiling them. I consider it wholly unnecessary.

Mashed potatoes are usually made from already cooked potatoes thinned out by milk and enriched with butter, but one can produce delicious mashed potatoes by boiling peeled potatoes in barely enough water to be absorbed in the cooking, adding a clove of garlic to every two potatoes and a teaspoon of cinnamon to every four. Boil until the potatoes are ready to dissolve in what is left of the water. Mash well, add $1/4$ to $1/2$ lb. butter, depending on the number of potatoes, salt, pepper, and parsley. Taste for cinnamon flavour. If not strong enough, add a little more. This is very good with the turkey on Christmas day. One can make masses of it and serve it easily. When I was a child, there was a yellow floury potato, very popular, called the Champion potato. It was always used for mashed potatoes, and we children used to call mashed potatoes 'champ'.

I like very much what I call *garlicky potatoes*. For this peel and slice the potatoes into enough water barely to cover and boil them to the point when they just begin to soften. Drain away any water that remains, always remembering to try and judge the water so that most of it is absorbed. Chop up finely two cloves of garlic, put them and a good knob of butter, salt, and pepper in with the potatoes, cover and finish cooking, looking from time to time to see that the bottom layer is not sticking to the pan. Sprinkle in the chopped-up parsley. A quick and savoursome way of cooking potatoes.

My mother used to do what she called *Virginian potatoes*. For this choose large potatoes, bake them until cooked, take out and cut one end off. Scoop out the flesh, mash and mix in butter, chopped parsley, thyme, salt and pepper, a little finely grated lemon peel, and a few drops of mushroom ketchup. Press back in the jackets and put back into the oven for a few minutes to heat up again.

Potatoes can be used in combinations with other vegetables and cheese to make sustaining dishes when meat is not available or not desired. Such is *Gratin of Potatoes and Mushrooms*.

Gratin of Potatoes and Mushrooms _____

Ingredients

2 lb waxy potatoes
$1/2$ lb mushrooms
$1/2$ cup finely chopped onions or shallots
$1/4$ cup chopped parsley

1 garlic clove finely chopped
$1/3$ cup Parmesan cheese
1 cup cream
2 tbsp butter
Salt and pepper

Method

Peel potatoes and slice them, place in a bowl of water while preparing the rest. Cut the mushrooms into thin slices and toss with onion, garlic, and parsley. Dry the potatoes and put them and the mushrooms in alternate layers in a well-buttered gratin dish, sprinkling the layers with cheese, butter, and seasoning. Finish with a layer of potatoes. Pour the cream over, then sprinkle with remaining cheese and dot with remaining butter. Bake at 325F, 110C, gas 3 for $1^1/2$ to $1^3/4$ hours.

A simple dish with a more aspiring title is *Johnson's Delight*.

Johnson's Delight _____

Ingredients

4 medium-sized potatoes
4 medium-sized onions
1 garlic cove finely chopped

$^1/_2$ pint cream
Salt, black pepper and parsley
  finely chopped

Method

Slice the potatoes and onions. Butter an oven-proof dish. Place the potatoes and onions in layers in the dish, finishing with potatoes. Season with salt and pepper and sprinkle the parsley and garlic over each layer. Pour over the cream. Cook at 350F, 190C, gas 5 for one hour.

    This recipe comes from my Swedish friend, whose name, Jansson, translates as 'Johnson' in English.

Another substantial potato dish is what the French call *Pommes aux Lardons*.

Pommes aux Lardons _____

Ingredients

$1^1/_2$ lbs potatoes
$1^1/_2$ lbs onions
2 oz pork fat
$^1/_2$ lb back bacon rashers

$^1/_2$ lb gruyère cheese (or
  cheddar)
$^3/_4$ pint of cream
Salt and black pepper

Method

Peel and slice finely the potatoes and the onions. Fry the onions in the pork fat until they are soft. Add the diced back bacon and continue frying for another 3 - 4 minutes. Grease a pie-dish, rub it with a cut clove of garlic and fill with alternate layers of potato and mixed onion and bacon, seasoning with salt and pepper and adding the thinly sliced cheese between the layers. Pour over the cream and bake in the oven at 350F, 180C, gas 4 for 40 - 45 minutes.

Salads

A salad can be made out of almost anything. The important part is the dressing. Good wine or cider vinegar and olive oil are essential, the degree of sharpness or blandness being determined by the proportion of vinegar to oil.

For a generally acceptable dressing I use the following:

Salad Dressing

Ingredients

1 measure of wine or cider
vinegar
4 measures of olive oil

1 clove of garlic
Salt and black pepper

Method

Crush the chopped-up garlic with $1/2$ tsp of salt. Add the vinegar and mix well. Next pour in the oil and stir until the mixture is amalgamated. Finally add the pepper and stir again. A little mustard powder may be blended in for material that requires added fierceness to balance the whole. For instance, tomatoes are the better for having their sweetness counteracted by the mustard, and so are potatoes.

Dandelion Salad

This is said to be the most popular winter salad in Greece.

Treat the dandelion leaves like spinach, cutting the stalks away and discarding the coarse outer leaves. Blanch them in boiling water for about 10 minutes. Drain well and dry. Tear the larger leaves up, put all into your salad bowl and pour over the dressing. Toss and serve. If you want to be authentically Greek, substitute lemon juice for the wine vinegar.

Lettuce and Grape Salad _____

I always add some green grapes to my lettuce salad. While they are to be found, use the seedless grapes, if not, you must de-seed them and cut in half. Toss in the dressing with the lettuce and a sprinkling of parsley, and if you like onions, with some finely sliced onion rings. There is a danger that you may get to feel that unanointed grapes are a bit tasteless.

Tangerine and Watercress _____

This is another unexpected combination.

Peel and divide the tangerines into sections. Wash the watercress thoroughly, dry and tear up. Toss in the oil and vinegar dressing.

I discovered this is Portugal one summer when there were plenty of tangerines and of watercress but little else that was green in the supermarkets.

Romaine Salad _____

Spinach is very good with raw mushrooms, and uncooked spinach goes much further than cooked. Remove the stalks of the spinach and slice the mushrooms very finely. Toss in the dressing and leave to marinate for a while.

Mushroom Salad _____

A plain mushroom salad must be made some hours in advance so that the mushrooms marinate in the dressing and release some of their juices. Use flat mushrooms, button mushrooms nowadays seem to be sold unripe. Clean the mushrooms with kitchen paper but do not wash. Cut off the stalks which can be used separately to flavour another dish. Slice finely and toss in the dressing. Scatter over some chopped parsley and chives just before serving. If you like, crisply fried and diced bacon may also be added.

Celery and Apple Salad _____

I had made salads of celery and apples long before I heard of Waldorf Salad which consists of these ingredients with the addition of finely chopped walnuts. For myself I can take or leave the walnuts and consider the apple and celery mixture very satisfactory.

Lorraine Salad _____

This is a mixture of celery and beetroot. The juice of the beetroot, which has been baked not boiled, turns the celery a pretty pink colour. But if you do not like beetroot, avoid it. The beetroot flavour tends to dominate.

Cabbage and Apple Salad _____

The inner leaves of York cabbage, very finely shredded, added to finely sliced apples makes a delicious salad. It should be prepared a few hours in advance so that the cabbage softens slightly.

Caesar Salad _____

This is an ordinary lettuce salad to which finely cut strips of ham have been added. If possible, use Cos lettuce for this.

Cooked Vegetable Salads _____

Some vegetables need to be cooked before being served as a salad. Such are leeks, cauliflowers and potatoes.

The **leeks** and **cauliflowers** should not be over-cooked, but kept *al dente* (ie slightly firm), and only the florets of the cauliflower and the white part of the leeks are used. Toss in the dressing while still warm.

Potato salad should also be made from quite warm potatoes. They should be peeled, sliced and tossed well in the dressing which can be sharper than usual. Just before serving add some mayonnaise and mix carefully. Sprinkle over finely chopped parsley and chives.

Tomato Salad

Tomatoes must be skinned. To do this place the tomatoes in a bowl and pour over boiling water. Count from 10 to 16 seconds, depending on their ripeness, lift out with a slotted spoon and remove skin. Cut crosswise and fold carefully into the dressing to which you have added a little mustard powder. Add some parsley and basil, fresh if possible, if not, dried.

Substantial Salads

A salad can be turned into a substantial dish by the addition of cheese or eggs, as with Greek Salad, or Salade Niçoise.

For the **Greek Salad** the vegetables used are tomatoes, cucumber, onion, green peppers, green and black olives. These, with the exception of the olives which are left whole, are cut up or sliced. They are then tossed in the oil and vinegar dressing, sprinkled with parsley and oregano and the whole topped with feta cheese cut into fairly big pieces. I think a good substitute for Greek feta, which may be difficult to find, is Cheshire, crumbly as it is.

Such a salad, with the addition of brown bread, followed by fruit, is sustaining enough for lunch on the odd occasion.

Salade Niçoise

A Salade Niçoise is even more sustaining. To a mixture of vegetables, including cooked potatoes, tomatoes, green or yellow peppers, beans and olives, are added hard boiled eggs and tuna fish on a bed of lettuce. The tuna fish forms the centre of the dish. The vegetables are arranged around it and the sliced or quartered eggs outside them and an oil and vinegar dressing poured over.

On a hot day in the south of France one does not ask for more at lunch, except fruit and coffee. It is, moreover, a dish that, when properly presented, looks very pretty and appetising.

Sauces and Stay-bites

People in a hurry cannot pause to make elaborate sauces and in many instances the cooking juices with a little lemon juice added will do very well as a sauce, provided a good cooking oil has been used. There are, however, some sauces that are very simple to make, cannot be omitted and can be done while the roast cooks.

Pork, for instance, must have *Apple Sauce* to accompany it.

Apple Sauce

Ingredients

2 large apples, Bramley
  Seedlings if available
1 tbsp water
1 tbsp sugar

Juice and rind of 1 lemon
  or, preferably, 1 lime
Knob of butter

Method

Peel, core and slice the apples into your saucepan: add the water and put over gentle heat. As soon as the apples begin to soften - which will be very soon - use a potato-masher to break them up. When they are pulped add the sugar and amalgamate. Stir in the rind and juice of the lemon or lime. If the lime is very small you may need another to get the correct sharpness. Never be tempted to add more sugar and do not overcook. Draw to the side of the cooker and just before serving heat up again and add a knob of butter: this will impart a lovely shine to the fruit. I discovered by accident that lime makes a better sauce.

This is also very good with turkey, by the way.

Béchamel Sauce

Ingredients

2 tbsp butter
3 tbsp flour
$1/2$ tsp salt

Dash of pepper
$1/4$ pt milk

Method

Melt the butter over a low heat. Sprinkle on the seasoned flour and stir carefully until you have a pale *roux*. Take off heat. Stir in the milk very gradually, beating with a wooden spoon to ensure smoothness. Continue stirring until the sauce is smooth and thick. If it seems too thick, add a little more milk.

This is the proper way to make a béchamel or white sauce. But when I was young, people in a hurry used to mix the flour with a little cold milk, add it to the rest of the milk and stir until it thickened over gentle heat, and then added the butter. If they were adding parsley they did this before the butter and cooked the parsley a little.

This white sauce was used as a basis for all kinds of sauces, known by the name of what was added - **Parsley, Caper** or **Onion. Caper Sauce** was served with boiled mutton. **Cheese Sauce** may be produced by adding grated cheese to the béchamel base. For serving with fish, mayonnaise may be added - but in this case do not boil the sauce after the mayonnaise has been added.

Egg and Lemon Sauce

Ingredients

2 eggs
Juice of 1 medium-sized lemon

$1/4$ pt of boiling stock from food in which it is to be used
(or chicken stock or cube)

Method

Beat the eggs with the lemon juice. Add the stock gradually, stirring constantly. Stir the sauce into the dish you intend to serve - or serve it as it is. **Do not let it boil.**

This is very good with fish.

Elderberry Jelly _____

This can be used as a sauce or as a condiment.

Ingredients

Enough elderberries to fill a
  large saucepan
Water to cover
Lemon juice in proportion
  (1 tbsp to the pint)

Ground ginger ($1/2$ tsp to every
  pint of fruit)

Method

Put the elderberries and water on to boil until juice is drawn. This takes longer than you would think, the elderberries being tough. Strain the liquid through a damp muslin (a very fine nylon sieve will do), allowing it to drip until all the juice has passed through. Reserve the liquid and measure it. To each pint add 1 tablespoon of lemon juice and $1/2$ teaspoon of ground ginger. To each pint of liquid allow a pound of *Sureset* sugar. Bring to a rolling boil for 1 minute. Cool and spoon into warmed clean jars. Cover and leave until Christmas.

This is delicious with the turkey or any game bird. You can also use it with ice-cream to make a delectable sweet confection.

Elderberries grow everywhere, but one has to be careful not to pick them from bushes exposed to dust or petrol fumes.

Mayonnaise

One Autumn many years ago, snatching a brief holiday, I was staying in Lerici in Italy: the lady of the house would sometimes invite one into the kitchen. She constantly made mayonnaise with just one egg and it never seemed to take her longer than a few minutes. Here is how she did it:

Ingredients

1 yolk of egg
$1/4$ pint olive oil
$1/2$ tsp lemon juice

Pinch of salt and white pepper
A crumb of white bread

Method

Dip the breadcrumb in lemon juice and rub the mixing bowl with it. Beat up the egg yolk, and add in, cautious drop by cautious drop, the olive oil, beating continuously. As the mixture thickens one can add more of the oil until all is used. Finally, slowly add the remaining lemon juice, the salt and the pepper.

Quantities may of course be increased proportionately, and the Mayonnaise may be made in a blender.

Tartare Sauce

Tartare Sauce is made by adding a few capers, chopped parsley and tarragon to a pint of Mayonnaise. A little finely chopped garlic improves the taste, I find.

Bread Sauce _____

Ingredients

2 oz fresh white fine
  breadcrumbs
$1/2$ onion stuck with 2 - 3 cloves
$1/2$ pint milk

1 oz butter
Salt and white pepper
Dash of cayenne pepper

Method

Simmer the onion and cloves in the milk until it is well
flavoured with them. Drain, then pour the milk over the
breadcrumbs, stir and bring back to the simmer. Draw to one
side of the cooker to allow breadcrumbs to swell and become
embued with the onion and clove flavours. Bring back to heat,
add the butter and mix well. Season to taste.

This is a classic accompaniment to roast pheasant and other
game. It is also often served with the Christmas turkey. For
myself, I can do without it. I like something more piquant with
my turkey, such as the *Elderberry Jelly* just described, or the
Apple Sauce, flavoured with lime and kept tart.

Mint Sauce _____

Ingredients

$1/2$ cup of fresh mint finely
  chopped
1 tbsp of sugar, white or brown

Enough boiling water to cover
  mint and allow it to infuse
2 - 3 tbsps wine vinegar

Method

Chop the mint very fine. Put it in your sauce-boat. Cover with
boiling water, add the sugar and leave to infuse. When it is
cold, stir well, add the vinegar, tasting after the second
tablespoon to see if more is needed. Stir well and leave aside
until needed. Just before serving, stir well.

Sorrel Sauce _____

Sorrel grows wild but the wild plant is a much smaller plant than the cultivated one. It is cooked like spinach but softens and turns into purée much more quickly. Use the purée as a filling for an omelette, or as a sauce with chicken or fish. In France cream, which has been previously boiled, is added slowly to the purée, but I prefer the pure sharp taste of the sorrel by itself.

I used to devour the wild sorrel leaves when I was a child: now I have it growing in my garden and it is the quickest of all sauces to make. I add a little ground coriander as well as salt and pepper in the cooking.

Stay-bites

Sometimes I used to tell my mother when I was very young that I was hungry but not for 'bread and butter'. We all know the condition when we want something to eat but a hunk of bread and cheese is not what we have in mind, nor is a full meal. Sudden attacks of unexplained hunger are more common in the young, but anyone can suffer them. What is required is something that satisfies the palate as well as the stomach. For immediate staunching of sudden hunger, mash a banana and mix it with a teaspoon or two of honey. If there is smoked salmon in the house, a slice or two, wrapped in a lettuce leaf that has been dipped in an oil and vinegar dressing will answer the purpose nicely. But failing that, here are some suggestions:

A Cheese Dip _____

Ingredients

$1/2$ lb cream cheese
1 - 2 tbsp lemon juice
1 tbsp fresh thyme finely
  chopped

1 tbsp parsley
1 small stick of celery *or* 1
  inner leaf of chicory
Salt and black pepper

Method

Beat the cream cheese and the lemon juice together: add the thyme and the parsley and mix well. Chop the celery or the chicory into minute pieces and amalgamate: make sure the celery or chicory is very finely diced. Season to taste with salt and pepper and beat all together.

    Spread some of this on a Bath Oliver or a Romary wheaten biscuit, or even any old water biscuit, and sudden hunger will be allayed. The crunchiness of the celery combined with the creaminess of the cheese is very satisfying.

French Toast _____

Ingredients

1 egg
4 slices of white bread or a fine
  brown bread

Pinch of cinnamon or nutmeg
Salt and pepper
Knob of butter

Method

Beat your egg: season it with salt, pepper and cinnamon or nutmeg. Cut the crusts off the bread and the bread into triangles, if you wish. Heat some butter in a frying pan to sizzling point: dip the bread into the egg and fry on both sides. If your frying pan is not big enough to do all the bread at once, add some more butter for the second lot. If any egg remains after dipping the bread into it, pour it on when you turn the slice over.

    Children usually love French Toast. Combined with rashers of bacon and a salad it makes a light meal. In this case use the bacon fat as well as the butter for frying the bread.

Apples and Cheese _____

Ingredients

4 eating apples - Cox's Orange
  or Worcester Pearmains, if
  available
Cashel blue cheese, about 2 oz
1 tbsp mayonnaise

1 tbsp cream
A little lemon juice
Parsley or tarragon
Salt and pepper

Method

Peel and core the apples. Dip in lemon juice to prevent
discolouration. Crush the cheese up, adding the tarragon or
parsley finely chopped. Mix in the mayonnaise, the whipped
cream, the lemon juice, the salt and pepper. Fill the cored
apples with the mixture and serve with cheese biscuits or
cream crackers.

Something similar can be done with **pears**. Cut them in
half, scooping out the centre. Fill the cavities with the mixture
but do not add any pepper. Serve as above.

Bacon and Sardine Toast _____

Ingredients

2 tbsp finely chopped
  cooked bacon

1 tin sardines
Slices of toast, as required

Method

Mash the bacon and the sardines together well. Spread the
mixture on the toast, cut into fingers, and heat through under
the grill or, if the oven is being used, in the oven.

Little Pizzas _____

Ingredients

Short crust pastry
  as on page 109

Tomato, onion and mushroom
  filling

Method

Cut out small circles of pastry with an egg-cup. Put on top of
each circle a filling made from tomato, onion and mushrooms,
either done fresh or one of the good brands now readily
available, and cook for 15 minutes in a 400F, 200C, gas 6
oven.

Potato Cakes _____

Ingredients

$1/_2$ lb hot mashed potatoes
$1/_2$ lb self-raising flour

3 oz butter
1 tsp salt

Method

Mix the potatoes, the flour and salt well together: rub in the
butter and knead well until a smooth dough results. Roll and
cut out into small rounds. Bake for 40 minutes in a 400F,
200C, gas 6 oven.
    Serve at once, split and buttered.
    Very satisfying, but only for those with a good digestion.

Puddings and Pies

Fruit

"I see some people are having ice cream for their pudding" said a delicately hinting little niece to me once when I had taken her out to lunch. For myself, I like fruit in some shape or form for my pudding.

The simplest of all preparations is fruit put to marinate in sugar and dry vermouth; or if one must be spartan, in sugar and lemon or orange juice. I hate cream baldly added to fruit: it masks the delicious tangy flavour of the juices. Oranges, though bitterer at some times of the year than at others, are never out of season. My version of the Italian *Arancia Straciata* is as follows:

Arancia Straciata

Ingredients

4 good-sized oranges   3 tbsps dry vermouth
2 - 3 tbsp brown sugar

Method

Dip the oranges in boiling water for a few minutes to make them easier to peel. Remove every particle of skin and pith. Slice crosswise against the sections and place in a glass bowl. Sprinkle the sugar over, varying the amount according to the sweetness of the oranges. Finally pour over the vermouth or lemon juice and leave to marinate for a couple of hours. Turn over carefully before serving. The juice from the oranges, the sugar and the vermouth combine to make a delicious liquor. Serve meringues with it if more substance is required or desired.

Strawberries lend themselves very well to this treatment. But use white caster sugar and do not leave too long or the strawberries will become sodden.

Another delicious combination is **white currants** and **raspberries**. Treat as for strawberries - an ethereal concoction!

But surprisingly, I think the most successful of all 'drunken fruits' are **blackberries**, free for the picking or available in our supermarkets. Use brown sugar with them and do not leave too long marinating. A plain sponge goes well with all summer berries. **Blackberries** also mix well with **melon**. They make a nice colour contrast together. After discarding the seeds of the half melon, scoop out some of the flesh, mix it with blackberries and return to the centre of the melon. Sprinkle on a little brown sugar and lemon juice, or dry vermouth.

If I had to have a summer berry straight, I should choose **raspberries**. Hilaire Belloc said of the strawberry:

Doubtless God could have made a better berry, but God never did.

I think God did. I think the raspberry is the better berry: it has a wilder, more woodlandy taste. They can grow wild too - I have picked them along the bank of a river. So does the strawberry too, of course, but such an atom of a fruit! One can never gather enough to satisfy, only to tantalise. When I was a child I transplanted some plants of wild strawberry to my grandmother's garden. Whether by inspiration or sheer accident, I put them in a rockery bed where the soil was apparently not too rich for them. They grew to twice their normal size. I know a sandy bank on an esker riada in County Offaly where they grow profusely.

Summer Pudding _____

A mixture of the summer berries - or any one kind - can make the classic Summer Pudding. This is made by lining a pudding bowl with slices of bread - or sponge cake - piling in a purée made from a mixture of white currants, red or black currants or blackberry alone and raspberries, putting a lid of bread or sponge on top, a plate on top of that and leaving long enough for the fruit to impregnate the bread or sponge. It may be turned out of the bowl or served in a bowl pretty enough to bring to table.

Fools

Fools are made from a purée of fruit - rhubarb, gooseberry, raspberry, blackberry, currants - and either whipped cream or a mixture of whipped cream and egg whites. Some people today substitute plain yoghurt for the cream, but I think the essence of a fool is the contrast between the bland and the thick and the tart and the thin, so I prefer to use cream.

I find that the **rhubarb purée** I make with marmalade and orange zest, which can be served as it is, also merges well with cream to make a fool with a difference. Here is the recipe:

Rhubarb Purée

Ingredients

6 sticks rhubarb
3 tbsp coarse-cut marmalade
1 tbsp water

Zest of 1 orange
Juice of 1 orange

Method

Slice rhubarb into inch-long pieces, put into saucepan with the water and marmalade. Bring to simmer, add zest of orange and cook until soft. If serving as it is, add the orange juice. If as basis of a fool, pour off excess juice, beat to a chiffon fineness and add whipped cream. No sugar is necessary: the marmalade sweetens it sufficiently. I sometimes float a few marshmallows on the top of the rhubarb mixture if I am serving it alone. It freezes well, I am told by my Swedish friend, who serves it in mid-winter with ice cream.

Rhubarb is easily grown: a few crowns of it in the garden is a great standby. My grandmother always had enough rhubarb forced by St Patrick's Day (17 March) to make a rhubarb tart. She put large up-turned earthenware pots over the selected crowns.

Jellies

Jellies made from packets are a favourite with children, but for real flavour they cannot equal jellies made from fresh fruit juices.

Try one of these:

Ingredients

$^1/_2$ pint strawberry, raspberry, loganberry or orange juice
$^1/_4$ lb caster sugar

1 dessertspoon lemon juice
$^1/_2$ oz gelatine

Method

Put the gelatine into a basin with $^1/_8$ pint of cold water and let it stand until it has soaked in the water then stir in $^1/_4$ pint of boiling water. Stir until the gelatine is dissolved. Sprinkle in the sugar, stir again and cool a little. Finally, add the selected fruit juice and pour into a wet mould or failing a mould, a pudding bowl. The taste will be the same!

A **lemon jelly** is made from less fruit juice - $^1/_4$ pint, and more boiling water - $^1/_2$ pint; or orange juice may be added to the lemon juice - $^1/_4$ pint - to ameliorate the tartness of the lemon.

Calf's Foot Jelly _____

In my grandmother's day this was the supreme luxury of the invalid. Here, for those who might like to sample it, is the recipe:

Ingredients

1 calf's foot, well washed and
   trimmed
1 oz caster sugar
Juice and zest of $1/_2$ lemon
1 white of egg, lightly beaten

Shell of egg, well washed
$1/_8$ packet of isinglass (jelling
   agent)
1 quart of cold water
1 wineglass of sherry

Method

Boil the calf's foot in the water until the liquor is reduced to half. Strain it into a basin and leave until cold and set. Remove every scrap of fat: to ensure this, pour a few tablespoons of boiling water over the jelly and float off the bits that come to the surface with kitchen paper. Put it back into a saucepan, leaving behind any sediment, add the strained juice and zest of the half lemon, the sugar, the sherry, the white of egg with the well-washed shell and the isinglass dissolved in a tablespoon of hot water and strained. Cook over gentle heat, stirring once or twice to dissolve the sugar, then bring to the boil and boil gently for 20 minutes, removing any scum that forms. Stand the saucepan at the side of the cooker and leave it for a quarter of an hour. Now strain it through a wet muslin or a jelly bag if you have one, or even a very fine nylon sieve. Stir only as much as necessary to dissolve the sugar; otherwise the jelly will be cloudy.

One used to be able to buy calf's foot jelly in a pharmacy, but it vanished from the shelves years ago.

Pastry

Pastry can be bought ready-made so easily nowadays that the art of making it at home may die out. But, once again, the home-made version is superior and a little practice enables one to produce the different varieties with ease.

The things to avoid in making pastry are using too much flour, rolling too hard, handling it too much and drowning it in water.

Puff Pastry _____

Ingredients

1/2 lb fine flour   1/2 tsp salt
1/2 lb butter

Method

Make sure your flour is perfectly dry - and your hands cold. Sieve the flour with the salt into a basin. Next mix the flour into a fairly soft dough with very cold water and be careful to use only as much water as is necessary. Knead the dough with your hands until it is smooth and velvety. Then turn it out on to a floured pastry board or slab, and roll it into an oblong about a 1/4 inch thick. Keep the edges neat.

Now put the butter into a clean lightly floured cloth and press it to remove all the moisture. Shape it into a neat square, pat, place in the middle of the dough, fold one side of the dough over the butter and the other side over that, so that you have three folds. Press the edges well together and turn the side with no edges to your right-hand side. Now roll the pastry out again and be careful to handle the rolling pin lightly for fear the butter might break through. Repeat this folding and rolling process seven times, always turning the pastry towards your right hand. At this point put the pastry away in a cold place for at least an hour, or overnight if you wish.

Take out and shape to required size. Puff pastry is particularly good for making mince pies or jam tarts and the cooking tins need not be greased.

Rough Puff Pastry

Ingredients

$1/2$ lb flour
$3/8$ lb butter
Juice of 1 lemon

1 tsp salt
Cold water

Method

Sieve the flour and salt into a basin. Chop the butter into the flour, either with a knife or pastry cutter, the butter taking on the size of walnuts. Make a hole in the middle of the mixture and pour in the lemon juice and about 2 tablespoons of water. Mix all into a paste using as little water as possible and not handling it at all but mixing with a palette or a broad-bladed knife. It should look like rough breadcrumbs at this stage. Gather it together and put on to the floured pastry board. Roll out.

Fold it in three, putting the side that has no edge at your right-hand side. Roll out into an oblong strip. Fold in three.

Repeat this folding and rolling twice more and it is ready for cooking. But best set aside for an hour.

Pastry for Pizzas

Ingredients

8 oz flour
5 - 6 oz lard

Pinch of salt
2 tsp water

Method

Put the lard into your mixing bowl with the salt and the water. Sift the flour over it. Cut the lard into the flour with a round-bladed knife or a pastry cutter, mixing as you cut. When the mixture looks like breadcrumbs, draw it together with your hand into a rough ball and at this stage put it away in a cold place for at least an hour. You can make it up to this point and leave it overnight or from morning until evening. Next, very lightly, and using only the tips of your fingers, press the sides of the paste to the middle until the ball is smooth. Dust your pastry board lightly with flour; do the same with your rolling pin and roll out the pastry with short quick rolls, lifting the pin at the end of each roll to keep the shape round, using the sides of your hand to smooth it between rollings.

Pizzas are made in Italy with bread dough, put into brick ovens with long-handled mallets and brought out piping hot. But this pastry makes not a bad substitute.

Puff pastry and Rough Puff should be baked in an oven pre-heated to 425F, 220C, gas 7. Pizza pastry in a 400F, 200C, gas 6 oven.

Short Crust Pastry

It is not so difficult to achieve success with this pastry and it is the usual one used to make pies and tarts.

Ingredients

8 oz self-raising flour   Pinch salt
4 oz butter   Ice-cold water

Method

Sift the flour and salt into a bowl, cut in the butter with a knife or pastry cutter, then rub it in with the tips of your fingers. When it is reduced to the consistency of fine breadcrumbs, make a hole in the middle and pour in a tablespoon of cold water. Gradually mix in the dry crumbs from the sides, adding more water as required, a teaspoon at a time. Put your hand to the mixture when it coheres, wiping it around the sides and bottom of the bowl. Knead as little as possible, roll out quickly and cook at once, with whatever filling you like, in a 400F, 200C, gas 6 oven for 45 minutes for an open tart.

French Pastry _____

This is made with an egg, and some people prefer it for pies and flans, holding that the other pastries get soggy from the filling.

Ingredients

8 oz flour	2 - 3 oz caster sugar
4 oz butter	1 egg

Method

Rub the butter into the sifted flour as described above. Beat the egg lightly and mix into flour. Gather up the dough and knead the caster sugar quickly into it on your pastry board. Cook it either in two sandwich tins or on one big pie plate in a 400F, 200C, gas 6 oven for about 1/2 hour. When it is cold fill it with the fruit of your choice, either cooked as with apples, or fresh berries, strawberries or raspberries or loganberries sweetened to taste and, if you wish, covered with a glaze made from a fruit jelly.

Pies and Tarts

The difference between pies and tarts is simply that pies are covered with pastry and tarts are left open. The berries are usually presented in the form of tarts, while solid fruits, such as apples and pears, which require cooking, are used for pies. Rhubarb is the first fruit of the year to appear and I give now the recipe for my version of *Rhubarb Tart*:

Rhubarb and Marmalade Tart _____

Ingredients

6 sticks of well-grown rhubarb
2 heaped tbsps marmalade

Zest and juice of 1 orange
1 tsp ground ginger

Method

Wash and wipe the rhubarb but do not peel it. Cut it up into $1/2$ inch pieces. Make half the quantity of short crust pastry described on page 109. Roll it out to fit a metal pie plate or Pyrex plate. Smear over a little marmalade. Arrange the rhubarb in concentric rings. Spread the marmalade over, add the grated zest of the orange, the ground ginger and a sprinkle of orange juice. Bake in a pre-heated 400F, 200C, gas 6 oven for 50 to 60 minutes. No sugar is necessary with this tart: the marmalade sweetens it enough and I find that the thin layer of marmalade on the pastry base prevents it from going soggy.

You can serve cream with this tart, if there are cream fanatics around, but I think it spoils the flavour. And, of course, you can use the French pastry as a base and cook the rhubarb separately, adding one to the other when both are cold. But with the short crust pastry you can serve the tart hot or cold.

Hesperides Pie _____

This pie is so called from the golden colour of the apples.

Ingredients

Short crust pastry as before
1$^1/_2$ lbs cooking apples
4 oz brown sugar

1 tbsp quince jelly or
  apricot jam
$^1/_2$ tsp nutmeg freshly grated

Method

Make the filling first. Peel, core and slice the apples. Put them, the sugar, the jelly or jam, and the nutmeg in a saucepan and cook until the apples are soft. Do not overcook. Let them cool. Make the short crust pastry. If you are using a pie plate, line it with a thin layer of pastry, spread a little apricot jam over, put in the fruit, roll out a slightly thicker circle for the top. Damp all around the edges of the lower layer, lay the top one on and punch the edges together.

Cook in a pre-heated 400F, 200C, gas 6 oven for 50 to 60 minutes.

Almond Tart _____

A luscious but not cloying confection.

Ingredients

Short crust pastry, half the
  amount given on page 109
4 oz butter
4 oz sugar

4 oz ground almonds
2 eggs
Few drops of ratafia essence

Method

Pre-heat oven to 400F, 200C, gas 6.

Beat the butter and sugar together over gentle heat; add the ground almonds and continue cooking for ten minutes. Beat the eggs lightly, add to the mixture and return to the heat for another five minutes. Finally, add in the ratafia essence. Roll out enough pastry to fit bottom and sides of a greased sandwich tin: spread a thin layer of apricot jam over the pastry. Spoon in the cooled almond mixture and smooth surface with broad-bladed knife. If there are any strips of pastry over make a lattice-work pattern on top of tart. Put in oven and cook for 50 to 60 minutes. I find that it takes the full hour to cook this tart: the filling should be firm to the touch.

If the top of any pie or tart cooks too quickly, put a piece of greased brown paper on top.

If preferred, the filling may be made with 2 oz ground almonds and 2 oz grated apple: then you have an **Almond and Apple tart**. All kinds of fillings may be used with the short crust base to make different kinds of tarts. A **Pear Tart** made from a purée of cooking pears flavoured with ground cinnamon, a **Banana and Sultana Tart**, a **Cherry Tart** made from cherries poached in claret with a hint of cinnamon, a **Gooseberry Tart** made from a pound of gooseberries stewed in as little water as possible, sieved and mixed with a knob of butter, a beaten egg, 2 oz breadcrumbs and sugar to taste, all piled into your short crust base.

In my grandmother's garden there were several different kinds of gooseberry, including one, a dessert gooseberry, that bore big, golden sweet fruit more delicious than grapes, I thought. There was also a green gooseberry with a skin so fine that it was transparent. I remember discovering that the hens, which occasionally escaped from their own quarters into the garden, liked eating gooseberries as much as we did. I reported this piece of natural history to the grown-ups: some days later I was stretched under a gooseberry bush with my arm thrust up the middle, plucking the ripe juicy fruit and popping it into my mouth; I was immersed in my greedy demolition, when I heard my aunt's voice say: "now I know the hens that are eating my gooseberries!" She had come silently through the long grass: I was absolutely discredited as a natural historian.

Gooseberry Custard Tart _____

Another kind of gooseberry tart where the fruit is covered with a custard and the tart taste is offset by the blandness of the custard.

Ingredients

Short crust pastry as for *Almond Tart*
1 lb gooseberries
3 oz sugar

$3/4$ pint cream
2 egg yolks
A little jam, apricot or gooseberry

Method

Pre-heat oven to 400F, 200C, gas 6.

Top and tail the gooseberries, spread the jam thinly on the pastry which you have put into a sandwich tin. Mix the cream, the sugar and the beaten egg yolks together. Arrange the gooseberries evenly on the pastry and pour the liquid over. Bake for 40 minutes until the custard is firm to the touch.

I think this tart is better served cold. In the winter, when gooseberries are out and seedless grapes are in, one may substitute grapes and produce a **Grape Tart**.

Upside-down Pudding _____

This is one of those puddings where the solid part consists of a sponge mixture.

Ingredients

Sponge
4 oz butter
4 oz sugar
6 oz flour, self raising
2 eggs
Juice and grated rind of 1 orange

Topping
Fresh, bottled or tinned fruit - apples, apricots, pears, cherries, gooseberries
A spice suitable to the fruit
Coating for pie dish
2 oz butter
3 oz brown sugar

Method

Pre-heat oven to 400F, 200C, gas 6.

Beat the 2 oz butter and the brown sugar together and coat the bottom and sides of the pie dish. Put in your prepared fruit. Now make your sponge: beat the 4 oz butter and sugar to a cream; add the beaten eggs slowly and carefully, if necessary sprinkling in a little flour in between. Fold in the rest of the flour. Add the grated rind and enough orange juice to make a soft mixture. Spoon over the fruit and cook for 50 to 60 minutes. When the sponge is firm to the touch, take out and turn on to a serving plate. The fruit will be on top with its buttery sugary coating, and the supporting sponge beneath.

Marmalade Bread Pudding _____

Ingredients

2 lbs white breadcrumbs
4 oz butter
4 oz sugar
2 oz sultanas
2 oz candied peel

2 eggs
$^1/_2$ pint milk
1 orange, rind and juice
4 tsp marmalade

Method

Cut the butter through the breadcrumbs: add all the dry ingredients. Beat the eggs. Bring the milk to the boil, mix in the egg and pour over, mixing thoroughly. Add the zest and juice of the orange and finally the marmalade, amalgamating well all components. Grease a pie-dish and spoon the pudding in, smoothing the surface. Bake in a 375F, 190C, gas 5 oven until the top is brown and crusty, about 1 hour.

Queen of Puddings _____

A simple bread pudding, given this extravagant name.
Children like it.

Ingredients

4 oz white breadcrumbs
2 oz sugar
$1/2$ oz butter
$1/2$ pint milk

1 egg
2 tsp jam
1 lemon, rind and juice
Vanilla flavouring

Method

Mix all dry ingredients together. Put milk and butter into a
saucepan and bring to the boil. Separate the yolk of the egg
from the white and beat it: add to the milk and pour over the
dry ingredients mixing well. Add the flavouring. Put into a
greased pie-dish and cook in a 375F, 190C, gas 5 oven until
set. Spread jam over the top and pile the stiffly beaten egg
whites on top. Put back into oven for a few minutes to set the
meringue.

Baked Lemon Suet Pudding
Birr Recipe _____

When I was a child in Birr, the winters were colder than they
are now. Besides, Birr enjoys, in relation to the rest of Ireland,
a continental climate. It is right in the middle of the country
and is always at least two degrees colder or warmer than
elsewhere. Suet puddings were popular in the winter. People
said they needed something to keep the life in them and the
cold out. I give the following recipe in my mother's words.

Ingredients and Method

4 oz suet, freed from skin and grated on to $1/2$ lb of fresh white
breadcrumbs and sweetened with 4 oz of sugar. As many
sultanas as seem agreeable are also stirred in and the grated

rind of a big moist lemon. The juice, cleared of pips, is added next, then the mixture stands while 4 eggs are broken into a bowl and beaten for five minutes. These are poured over the dry things and the lot is blended into an even, smooth whole. Bake in a buttered pie-dish for an hour in a fairly brisk oven. (I suggest 400F, 200C, gas 6, lowering to 5 if it seems to be cooking too quickly - the suet used is, of course, beef suet).

Apple Dumpling
Another Winter recipe

Ingredients

4 oz self-raising flour
2 oz finely chopped suet
2 oz fine bread crumbs
Pinch of salt

2 large cooking apples
2 tbsp brown sugar, demerara or
  muscovado
Pinch of powdered cloves or
  cinnamon
Grated rind of lemon

Method

Put the sifted flour, breadcrumbs and suet into mixing bowl and stir well. Add just enough water, about three tablespoons, to make a stiff dough. Turn on to pastry board, lightly floured, and knead just enough to make dough cling together.

Grease a 6" deep pudding bowl and dust over with brown sugar. Cut off one-third of the dough, roll the rest out into a large round to line the bowl. Add the peeled, cored and sliced apple, the sugar, the rind of the lemon, the pinch of cloves or cinnamon. Wet the edges of the dough. Roll out the remaining pastry to cover the bowl and press the edges well together. Put a deep pleat in a sheet of greased paper. Cover bowl and tie down securely. Steam in a pan of boiling water for two hours or pre-steam for ten minutes in a pressure cooker, followed by 40 minutes at low pressure.

Lemon Soufflé Pudding _____

Ingredients

2 oz caster sugar
2 oz butter
4 oz flour

2 eggs
$1/4$ pint of milk
Juice and rind of 1 large lemon

Method

Pre-heat oven to 350F, 180C, gas 4. Cream butter and sugar, add rind and juice of lemon carefully, combine with flour. Add yolks and whites of eggs beaten separately. Put into greased baking dish, stand in a pan of cold water and bake for $3/4$ hour. The cooked pudding will have expanded into a spongy topping and a lemony sauce underneath.

Lemon Soufflé Pudding
Another Version _____

Ingredients

$1/2$ lb self-raising flour
$3/4$ lb butter
$3/4$ lb caster sugar
6 eggs

$1\frac{1}{2}$ lemons, grated rind
  and juice
2 tbsp brandy

Method

Cream the butter and sugar together. Add the beaten yolks of eggs. Fold in the flour and the lemon rind. Add lemon juice and the egg mixture alternately to the flour. Add the brandy and finally the whites of the eggs beaten to two stiff peaks. Bake for $1\frac{1}{2}$ hours in gas 4, 350F, 180C. Enough for a party.

Teatime Treats

When I was growing up and people had more time to spare they constantly 'whipped up' a sponge or 'slapped' up a Sally Lunn for tea. They entertained one another to tea then too, as few of us do nowadays. Still, a classic sponge cake takes very little time to prepare and cook, especially if you have an electric mixer.

Classic Sponge

Ingredients

4 oz flour with $1/2$ tsp salt added
4 oz caster sugar

4 eggs, in weight 4 oz
Flavouring - vanilla, ratafia, lemon etc

Method

Pre-heat oven to 400F, 200C, gas 6.

Beat the eggs to a creamy froth; add the sugar gradually, beating continuously. Now fold in the sifted flour very carefully and lightly. Have ready two well-greased sandwich tins. Sprinkle the bottom with a thin layer of flour and caster sugar mixed. Divide the sponge between them and bake in the centre of the oven for 8 - 10 minutes. Take up, leave for a few minutes before turning on to a wire rack to cool. Before they are cold, put together with a thick layer of lemon curd or raspberry jam, home-made if possible, between. Raspberry is the classic accompaniment but I much prefer lemon curd. The success of a sponge like this depends on the beating and the incorporation of air bubbles in the mixture. Such a sponge does not keep: it must be eaten at once. If you want one for keeping, make a Victoria sponge.

Sally Lunn

Ingredients

$^1/_2$ lb fine flour, sifted
1 oz butter
$^1/_2$ oz yeast
About $^1/_4$ pint lukewarm milk

1 egg, well beaten
1 dessertspoon caster sugar
$^1/_2$ tsp salt

Method

Pre-heat oven to 375F, 190C, gas 5. Melt the butter in a saucepan, add the milk and let it warm but not approach boiling point. Cream the sugar and the yeast together and add some of the milk and butter. Make a hole in the centre of the flour and pour the liquid in. Mix into a smooth dough adding the beaten egg and the remainder of the milk and butter. Use a wooden spoon to amalgamate all together. Wrap in a cloth and leave in a warm place for an hour to rise. Put into a well-greased tin and bake for about $^3/_4$ hour. Glaze with a sugar and milk glaze made from a dessertspoon of white sugar dissolved in a dessertspoon of warm milk. Serve warm.

Almond Scones _____

Ingredients

4 oz self-raising flour with 1 tsp
  salt added
2 oz butter
2 oz ground almonds
2 oz sultanas

2 oz mixed candied peel
  (optional)
4 oz sugar
1 egg beaten
Juice of 1 orange

Method

Pre-heat oven to 400F, 200C, gas 6.

Sieve the flour and salt into a mixing bowl: rub the butter
in, add all the other dry ingredients and mix well. Beat the egg
and squeeze the orange. Add the egg to the mixture beating
well; finally add the orange juice to obtain a soft but not
sloppy dough. Turn out onto a floured board and roll out about
1 inch thick. Use a sherry glass to cut out into round shapes.
Put your scones on a floured baking sheet or greased and
floured flat dish and bake for 20 minutes or until firm to the
touch. Serve warm. These scones need neither butter nor jam:
they are very rich.

Hot Muffins _____

Ingredients

1 lb self-raising flour
$1/2$ pint cream

1 tsp salt
2 tsp sugar

Method

Pre-heat oven to 400F, 200C, gas 6.

Sieve the flour and salt, add the sugar and mix well. Make
into a dough with the cream; do this as quickly and lightly as
possible. Roll out on a floured board to a thickness of $1/2$ inch.
Cut into circles about $2^1/2$ inches in diameter. Put into the
oven and cook from 5 to 10 minutes.

Divide in two, butter them and serve at once.

Macaroons _____

Ingredients

4 oz ground almonds
4 oz white sugar
Whites of two large eggs

Almond essence to taste
Rice paper

Method

Pre-heat oven to 325F, 160C, gas 3.

Mix the sugar and ground almonds together, adding the essence to taste. Fold in the whipped white of eggs. Lay out your rice paper and put teaspoons of the mixture on it. Bake for about 20 minutes to a pale yellow colour. Remove the surplus rice paper and store when cold. Delicious morsels as they are, some people prefer the taste of the bitter almond and flavour them with ratafia.

Caraway Cake _____

If you like the flavour of caraway seeds, you will like this. For some reason caraway has gone out of fashion: I am addicted to it myself.

Ingredients

8 oz self-raising flour
6 oz white sugar
4 oz butter
1 egg

1 oz caraway seeds
A pinch of salt
Milk to mix

Method

Pre-heat oven to 360F, 175C, gas 4.

Rub the butter into the flour. Add the sugar, the caraway seeds and a pinch of salt. Mix well. Beat the eggs, add a little milk and stir it into the mixture which should be rather soft. Have ready a one-pound well-greased cake tin. Pour the mixture in and bake for 1 hour. When ready, take out of the tin and allow to cool on a wire rack.

Almond and Carrot Cake _____

I think this goes back to the Birr of my childhood, and the circle of ladies there who exchanged recipes.

Ingredients

8 oz carrots
5 oz ground almonds
5 oz caster sugar
2 oz wholemeal flour

$^1/_2$ tsp baking powder
1 tsp ground mixed spice
1 lemon
3 eggs

Method

Pre-heat oven to 350F, 180C, gas 4. Peel the carrot, remove rind of lemon, grate both finely. Separate the yolks and whites of eggs. Whisk the yolks and sugar well together. Stir in carrots, almonds and lemon rind. Shake in flour sifted with baking powder. Add spices. Finally whip white of eggs and fold into mixture. Spoon into cake tin and bake for 45-50 minutes.

State Days and
Bonfire Nights

Recipes for Christmas, Hallowe'en, Shrove Tuesday and other 'State Occasions'

Christmas

Roast Turkey

Ingredients

1 turkey 10 - 12 lbs
Stuffing for the body
Stuffing for the craw
1/2 bottle of dry white or red
  wine

4 oz butter
Parsley and tarragon
Lemon juice

Method

Pre-heat oven to 400F, 200C, gas 6.

Turkey is a dry bird, so it needs to be well lubricated in the cooking and encased in either a roasting bag or aluminium foil. If you put it in a bag, you will not be able to add wine or stock, but if you use foil, you can add stock or wine and ensure that the flesh is kept moist.

Use a bread and whiskey stuffing, as for pork steaks (page 61) but in quantity sufficient to fill the body of the bird. Stuff the craw with sausage meat, seasoned with salt and black pepper or a mixture of sausage meat and unsweetened chestnuts, fresh if you want to give yourself extra trouble, but just as good out of a tin.

Smear the breast and thighs with butter into which the chopped parsley, tarragon and lemon juice have been amalgamated. Heat the wine or stock and pour into the pan around the bird up to about 2 inches. Put a covering of foil all over with the ends inside the pan. Put into oven and cook for about 40 minutes. Lower heat to 350F, 180C, gas 4 and cook for 20 minutes to the lb, topping up with wine when necessary and making sure foil remains in place. If you think your turkey is cooking too quickly, lower heat, and take a little longer time to finish it off. When you look to see if wine needs topping up, baste the bird well. It should come out moist and succulent. The cooking juices are enough in themselves for a gravy.

Steamed Christmas Cake

Ingredients

1 lb raisins
1 lb sultanas
$^1/_2$ lb currants
$^1/_4$ lb ground almonds
$^1/_4$ lb candied peel
$^3/_4$ lb cherries

$^1/_2$ nutmeg grated
14 oz flour
$^1/_2$ tsp bread soda
4 eggs
4 tbsp whiskey
2 tbsp buttermilk

Method

Cream butter and sugar, add eggs one by one, continuing to beat well. Mix all dry ingredients together and fold into creamed mixture. Mix bread soda and buttermilk till it froths. Fold into mixture. Finally mix in whiskey. Put into well-greased tin, cover with greased paper. Have ready large pot with boiling water one inch in depth. Place tin in this and steam for $1^1/_2$ hours, adding more water from time to time as it boils away. Pre-heat oven to 325F 170C, gas 3, and bake cake for a further two hours.

This is a luscious moist cake but needs careful cooking. Ice in the usual way, first with marzipan and then with white icing.

Porter Cake

This is a sharp-tasting cake for those who find the usual Christmas baking too cloying.

Ingredients

1 lb raisins
1 lb currants
1 lb caster sugar
$1/4$ candied peel
$1/2$ lb butter
4 eggs

1 tbsp mixed spice
1 lb flour
1 tsp bread soda
1 tsp salt
$1/2$ pint porter

Method

Pre-heat oven to 325F, 170C, gas 3 oven. Cut butter into salted sieved flour, add other dry ingredients. Beat the eggs and add the porter, combine with dry ingredients and beat well for ten minutes. Line tin with greased paper and bake for $2^{1}/_{2}$ to 3 hours.

Another rough textured but well-flavoured cake. I should add that this is a very old recipe, inherited by my mother from a first cousin once-removed.

Plum Pudding

Ingredients

1 lb raisins
$1^{1}/_{2}$ lb sultanas
1 lb currants
$1^{1}/_{2}$ lbs demerara sugar
1 lb butter
$3/4$ lb of sieved self-raising flour
  and 1 tsp salt
1 lb fine breadcrumbs fresh
$1/4$ lb ground almonds

2 apples grated
$1/4$ lb mixed peel
$1/4$ lb crystallized cherries
1 large lemon, rind and juice
$1/2$ tsp cinnamon, cloves, and
  mixed spice
6 eggs
4 tbsp whiskey
1 bottle Guinness

Method

Mix all dry ingredients except the spices. Add eggs beaten with the Guinness, add whiskey and lemon juice and finally the spices. Stir all well together. Cover with clean cloth and leave overnight (when I was a child, everybody in the house was expected to give a few stirs to the pudding). Next day mix again, put into well-greased pudding bowls and boil for six hours. Reboil for a further two hours before serving.

Accompany pudding with *Guards' Sauce* - equal quantities of butter and sugar beaten together, then infiltrated with brandy or mixed with quantities of sherry and whiskey and finally sprinkled with ground nutmeg. This should be made a few hours beforehand and left in a cool place to harden.

Never serve cream with plum pudding; it offers no contrast in texture. This sauce is supposed to have acquired its name from the Guards' Mess to which it was introduced at the time of the Fenian Rising in Canada. In my young days, slices of left-over plum pudding were sometimes fried in butter on Stephen's Day instead of being eaten cold.

Serve a Gewürtztraminer wih the plum pudding.

Last Minute Plum Pudding _____

This is the plum pudding my aunt used to make. She never believed in making puddings weeks in advance: she was a very busy woman and had her own methods of dealing with life's exigencies. She maintained that a chicken could be killed, plucked warm, and cooked at once, instead of following the usual custom of killing it a few days before it was needed.

Ingredients

4 oz raisins
4 oz sultanas
8 oz currants
8 oz self-raising flour
8 oz breadcrumbs
8 oz grated carrots
8 oz grated apples
8 oz brown sugar

6 oz beef suet, or butter
$1/2$ nutmeg, grated
1 tsp mixed spice
1 tbsp marmalade
1 tbsp golden syrup
$1/4$ pint Guinness
2 eggs well-beaten

Method

Mix all dry ingredients together, stir the liquid ones together and then combine all into a mixture of soft dropping consistency. If more liquid is required, stir in a little whiskey. Grease well two 8" pudding basins or four smaller ones. Divide mixture between them. Cover first with greased paper and then with foil, secure and boil for six hours. Remove covering, leave to cool and re-cover. Boil for a further two hours on Christmas Day or whenever you serve it.

This plum pudding has the advantage that it doesn't need to be made months in advance although it tastes very good indeed.

Hallowe'en

Hallowe'en, also known as the eve of All Saints, is celebrated on 31 October.

Colcannon, and apples in every shape and size, were traditional at Hallowe'en. Barmbracks too and games with apples, such as snap-apple.

Colcannon

Colcannon is properly made with equal quantities of kale and potatoes, but in my childhood cabbage was often substituted, since it was easy to find and some people preferred its taste. The potatoes must be well mashed and seasoned with salt, pepper and cinnamon, or nutmeg. The kale is prepared like spinach, boiled in as little water as possible, chopped up and beaten chiffon-fine.

A couple of leeks should be boiled in milk until soft and added to the potatoes with sufficient milk to result in a malleable purée. Kale and potatoes are then whipped together over gentle heat until well amalgamated. Butter may be added, as you wish, or melted and poured into the middle of the purée. With the addition of fried rashers it makes a solid meal.

Apple tarts were always made for the feast, and **baked apples** which were eaten late at night with caster sugar and whipped cream. I remember the wrinkled skins of the apples and their chewiness contrasting with the soft pulp of the flesh. The Winter Russets were not yet ripe, so Allington Pippins were used instead. They are a yellow and rose-skinned apple.

One of my uncles always made a great fuss of Hallowe'en. We were invited to his house for the evening. There were tubs of water with apples in them from which ourselves and our cousins were supposed to snatch an apple in our teeth. There were apples suspended from the ceiling which again one was expected to bite at. There were nuts, put to roast on the coals, and all kinds of portents were indicated from the way they flew. Lighted candles were attached to a sort of wooden chandelier hanging from the ceiling and twirled around. I once set fire to myself by leaning too far backwards over a candle, but my aunt, never fazed by anything that could happen to a child, and constantly called on to push down our throats boiled sweets that had lodged there, seized me and slapped out the flames with her hand.

The **barmbracks** were solid concoctions made with yeast, but anything made with yeast takes a long time in the preparation so try the following substitute. You can add the traditional brass ring and the silver coin if you like.

Tea Bread

Ingredients

8 oz self-raising flour
4 oz demerara sugar
12 oz sultanas
2 oz walnuts chopped up

1 egg beaten
$1/4$ pint strong tea
3 tbsp sherry or whiskey

Method

Pre-heat oven to 350F, 180C, gas 4. Place sultanas and sugar in a bowl. Pour over the cold tea and the sherry or whiskey and leave overnight. Next day add dry ingredients and the egg and beat well. Turn into a well-greased loaf tin 7" x 4" and bake for 1¼ hours. If the top browns too quickly place a sheet of greased brown paper over it. The flavour varies according to the tea used and what kind of alcohol is added.

All kinds of spooky stories were told at Hallowe'en, stories about the Pooka who was abroad on that night, about headless coaches and fairy-rings into which people blundered and wandered around, not able to get out. The big black dog that was supposed to haunt the 'Black Sticks', the remains of the paling that surrounded the site of the church built by the people of Birr for the schismatic priest who commanded their allegiance at one time, also made his appearance on All Hallows night. It was a delightful sensation to be made shivery by the thought of such supernatural manifestations but not really to be afraid. One was safe in the ordinary world, looking through a gateway at strange possibilities. All the same, when the time came to leave our cousins, the others huddled around me and we flew home.

Shrove Tuesday

Shrove Tuesday, also known simply as Pancake Day, is the Tuesday immediately before Ash Wednesday which marks the beginning of Lent, a period of fasting, in the Christian tradition.

Pancakes were the order of the day for Shrove Tuesday, pancakes or fritters. The basis of both is the same: a batter, thinner for pancakes, thicker for fritters. But the same methods apply to both. First the eggs used must be fresh, next the batter must be thoroughly beaten either by hand or by a food processor. The flour must be added slowly so that a smooth blend is ensured and finally the batter must be made at least an hour beforehand and left to stand. It is better still to leave it longer. A special pan, enamel if possible, should be kept for pancakes.

Pancake Batter _____

Ingredients

$1/4$ lb flour
2 eggs

$1/2$ pint milk
$1/2$ oz butter

Method

Whisk the yolks of the eggs for 5 minutes, then whisk the whites until they form a stiff froth. Add a tablespoon of milk to the yolks and mix them. Beat in a dessertspoonful of flour. Proceed alternately like this with the milk and the flour, beating continuously. Stir in the whipped white of eggs and leave for one or two hours. Beat up again, before cooking. Heat your frying pan, melt a little butter and when it is hot, slide in enough of your batter barely to cover the pan. Leave for two or three minutes, then loosen the edges and either turn with a palette knife or toss. If you use a small pan, it will be easy to toss the pancake. Continue until you have used up the batter, adding a little more butter as necessary. Drain the pancakes on kitchen paper. Sprinkle with caster sugar, roll up and serve with plenty of lemon juice squeezed over. Keep the cooked ones warm over a pan of hot water while you cook the others.

Batter for Fritters _____

Ingredients

$1/2$ lb flour
$1/2$ oz of butter
$1/2$ pint of milk

2 eggs
A good pinch of salt.

Method

Sift the flour and salt. Whisk the eggs well and beat them into the flour. Melt the butter and mix it with the flour and eggs. Next add the milk, slowly, beating all the time and being careful not to make the batter too thin. It must be thicker than a pancake batter but thin enough to drop from the spoon.

This batter can be used to make apple fritters or banana or pineapple fritters.

For **apple** fritters choose firm cooking apples. Peel, core and cut them crosswise into slices, sprinkle with white sugar and then with lemon juice and let them stand for over an hour. Immerse the slices in the batter, take out and place in sizzling butter or lard in pan and fry a golden brown. Sift caster sugar over and eat at once. Fritters should not be left; they become leathery. Ideally speaking, the recipients should be seated at table impatiently waiting.

Bananas are quartered, sugared, lemon-juiced and done in the same way.

Pound Cake

I have no idea why this is called 'Pound' cake, but it was often made at Easter, slightly less rich than the usual Christmas cake, and much enjoyed.

Ingredients

$1/2$ lb butter
$1/2$ lb caster sugar
9 oz self-raising flour
$1/2$ lb currants
$1/2$ lb sultanas
$1/4$ lb raisins

$1/4$ lb candied peel
2 oz cherries
2 oz slivered almonds
4 large eggs
Grated rind of half a lemon
$1/2$ glass of whiskey or rum

Method

Pre-heat oven to 350F, 180C, gas 4.

Beat butter and sugar to a soft cream, with the lemon rind. Add the eggs one at a time, beating until the mixture thickens again after each egg. Sift flour and fold lightly in. Mix fruit peel and almonds together and fold in. Turn into well-greased baking tin and sprinkle a few slivers of almond on top. Bake for $2^1/2$ hours. Pour the whiskey or rum over the cake while it is still hot.

Index